Transforming Professional Practice

Transforming Professional Practice

A Framework for Effective Leadership

Kimberly T. Strike, Paul Sims,
Susan L. Mann, and Robert Wilhite

ROWMAN & LITTLEFIELD
Lanham • Boulder • New York • London

Published by Rowman & Littlefield
An imprint of The Rowman & Littlefield Publishing Group, Inc.
4501 Forbes Boulevard, Suite 200, Lanham, Maryland 20706
www.rowman.com

6 Tinworth Street, London SE11 5AL, United Kingdom

British Library Cataloguing in Publication Information Available

Library of Congress Control Number: 2019950131

ISBN 978-1-4758-5301-8 (cloth : alk. paper)
ISBN 978-1-4758-5302-5 (paper : alk. paper)
ISBN 978-1-4758-5303-2 (electronic)

♾™ The paper used in this publication meets the minimum requirements of American
National Standard for Information Sciences—Permanence of Paper for Printed Library
Materials, ANSI/NISO Z39.48-1992.

Contents

~

Foreword

The genesis of this book evolved from the authors' conversation with Charlotte Danielson, who suggested that her research on *effective teaching* as seen in her 2007 book, *Enhancing Professional Practice: A Framework for Teaching*, could be the springboard for expanding the leadership field by exploring *effective leadership*. The demands for school improvement and reform require attention to a variety of innovative leadership behaviors, which include evaluation, supervision, mentoring, coaching, and professional growth. You can find support for these suppositions in the seminal work by Heifetz and Linsky, *Leadership on the Line: Staying Alive Through the Dangers of Leading*, in their model of adaptive leadership, which challenges each stakeholder in the school community to face complex educational demands. These challenges require board members, administrators, teachers, staff, students, community members, and organizations to learn and adapt new ways of engaging in shared leadership opportunities.

For every child to achieve his or her full potential and for educators to engage in meaningful professional learning require leadership approaches involving school communities in change that challenges their daily habits, loyalties, ways of thinking, and actions. This very challenge is acknowledged and supported in *Transforming Professional Practice: A Framework for Effective Leadership, Second Edition*, through its logical and user-friendly format, which emphasizes the requisite skills, dispositions, traits, and best practices for current and emerging school leaders to model in their leadership responsibilities within their respective districts and schools.

In this updated second edition, the authors created a blueprint for educational leaders to arrive at an understanding of the complexity of shared leadership for achieving reflective school improvement. The dispositions for leadership success are embedded in the Professional Standards for Educational Leaders (PSEL, 2015) created by the National Policy Board for Educational Administration (NPBEA) and the NELP standards (2018) created by a committee for National Educational Leadership Preparation approved by the Council for the Accreditation of Educator Preparation (CAEP). The NELP and PSEL standards are aligned to provide specificity around performance expectations for beginning level and district leaders. To support these key standards, *Transforming Professional Practice: A Framework for Effective Leadership, Second Edition*, advances the educational conversation by its keen focus on effective professional growth and development. This framework recognizes that the uniqueness of school leadership, whether at the central office level, school building level, or department level, is dependent on effective leaders who are self-reflective and developmentally attuned to professional growth opportunities.

The reader is treated to an exceptional set of new learning tools as the authors guide the reader through their chapters. They set the stage for the leadership framework, take the reader through the framework from Domains 1 through 4, examine effective leadership through professional learning, and describe how to use the leadership framework in supervision and evaluation. The framework accentuates the essential underpinnings of how to effectively lead and engage a school community effectively through a repertoire of activities and rubrics for the supervision, evaluation, and professional growth of its leaders.

These professional learning tools are further detailed in the appendix of the four domains that support the leadership framework: Domain 1—*Leadership Competencies*; Domain 2—*Professional Learning and Growth*; Domain 3—*Instructional Practices*; and Domain 4—*Management Competencies*. They serve as identifiers for educational leaders, whether experienced or aspiring, as a set of crafted ideas to bridge personal strengths and to acknowledge those areas that may support them in continuous professional learning and growth. Further, the authors have included a short case study at the end of each chapter with a series of probing questions to challenge the reader's working knowledge of the chapter's message and application.

Strike, Wilhite, Sims, and Mann have applied their unique professional experiences in shaping a remarkable set of benchmarks for educational leaders at all levels and stages to strive for a pragmatic approach to their supervisory and evaluative roles. The writing throughout this book is comfortable, clear, compelling, and mindful of guiding the reader in the many ways we as individuals and leaders touch and influence those around us. They give a powerful and authentic voice to the leadership field in expressing the importance of self-reflection in one's daily practice of ensuring school improvement and the enhancement of student learning by not going it alone but, rather, through collaboration.

Finally, this book looks to the potential for change. Problems exist, but they don't exist in isolation; they exist in human endeavors and can be dealt with through human partnerships and human efforts. The authors create a dialogue that invites us to engage in the process of thinking with them.

L. Arthur Safer, PhD
Professor Emeritus
Leadership and Policy Studies
Loyola University Chicago

Preface

The process of evaluation and supervision of teachers has evolved, as evidenced in practice as well as review of literature. In contrast, the evaluation and supervision of those in leadership roles remains underdeveloped and calls for both substantial improvement and specific direction. Those serving directly in leadership positions have an idea of what good leadership is and what the expectations are through standards such as PSEL (2015), NELP (2018), Learning Forward, or individual state standards from departments or offices of public instruction.

Although national and state standards serve as guidelines, those charged with supervision and evaluation of leaders have been left to create their own evaluation tools, rating scales, or methods of feedback. This practice has presented challenges, such as interrater reliability and credibility, from district to district. Lack of a common and accepted evaluation tool may even carry legal implications. For example, a district may have to keep a person in a leadership position due to a lack of evidence or a credible evaluation tool that allows for legal protections, such as due process and time frames for improvement. In addition, the leader may file a grievance or lawsuit if the evaluation is untimely, subjective, or not evidence based.

We have witnessed and participated in the process of supervision and evaluation. We are practitioners anchored in the theories of leadership. Approached and encouraged by colleagues serving in leadership roles, we were called to demystify the evaluation process for educational leaders. Through the exploration of knowledge, skills, dispositions, and practices of leadership recognized as effective, we developed the basis for this book, hereafter referred to as *The Leadership Framework*.

It is essential to have multiple points of view in order to address challenges encountered in the field. The resource must meet the needs of multiple users, serving in multiple roles, in multiple districts, each having its own culture and needs, regardless of the type of school. The knowledge, skills, dispositions, and practices identified in *The Leadership Framework* are required whether the school is public, parochial, charter, magnet, choice, or private. Regardless of the type of school, the leaders of the school and district must demonstrate that they are effective in their role, and those charged with their supervision and evaluation must be held accountable. The importance of district or school leadership should not be underrated.

Through personal experience and interaction with hundreds of educators in the field, we understand the social complexity, dynamics of the infrastructure, impact of critical issues and initiatives, pursuit of moral purpose, call for engagement in reflection, and process of supervision and evaluation. Related literature demonstrates the ambiguity of resources focused on supervision and evaluation of educational leaders. We have combined theory and practice with the development of a meaningful, action-based resource, *The Leadership Framework*.

This resource removes the ambiguity, demystifying the process of supervision and evaluation of educational leaders. It is important to note that we developed the resource with professional learning and growth as the goal. The resource provides the framework and defines specific expectations; however, the uniqueness of the individual setting is a critical factor that must be taken into account.

The successful use of this resource is dependent on the change process identified by Fullan (2007): initiation, implementation, and institutionalization (p. 66). In this case, initiation will need to include more than a mere adoption of the resource or superficial changes. Instead, there must be structural changes in culture and role along with careful consideration of goals and implications.

The process of implementation calls for pressure, support, and follow-through. Throughout the process, considerations of factors that have emerged (planned or unplanned), professional discussions focused on practices, and examination of goals must be ongoing. "Success . . . will depend on the degree and quality of change in actual practice" (Fullan, 2007, p. 85). Fullan goes on to say, "Whether or not implementation occurs will depend on the congruence between the reforms and local needs, and how the changes are introduced and followed through" (p. 99).

Institutionalization refers to whether the change becomes part of the integral workings or eventually dies out due to decision or as a result of attrition. In order to sustain the process of supervision and evaluation of leadership, it must be embedded through, among other things, policy, budget, established process, and timelines. It also must have those accountable for the supervision and evaluation of educational leaders, as well as the educational leaders themselves, be well informed, trained, and committed to the process.

In addition, procedures must be established so that, if or when there is a change in leadership, the process is well understood. Sustainability calls for leaders to develop other leaders. Finally, those entering district/school roles that call for understanding of the supervision and evaluation process must be provided training and orientation as well as ongoing support. This may include administrators new to the role, newly placed administrators, board members, peer reviewers, or other roles as identified within the district.

The organization of this book has been designed to share a tool with specific targets and provide common language to clarify the knowledge, skills, dispositions, and practices of effective educational leaders. The targeted audiences are those charged with the supervision and evaluation of leaders, current educational leaders, and aspiring leaders. Each chapter provides foundational information, case studies and reflective self-assessment as part of the process of understanding and actively participating in not only supervision and evaluation but also professional growth. Each chapter focuses on a part of the whole, and together they create a complete, comprehensive picture of effective leadership. In reading the book in its entirety, the reader connects leadership standards, leadership theories, and practices of effective leaders.

References

Fullan, M. (2007). *The new meaning of educational change.* (4th ed.). New York, NY: Teachers College Press.

~

Acknowledgments

We are grateful to the many people who have taught us how to be effective leaders who transform our professional practice. As leaders, our journey is continuous as well, for "the moment you stop learning, you stop leading" (Maxwell, 2007, p. 1365).

To our students, we offer thanks for challenging us to be role models and encouraging and supporting us in our publications, presentations, and teaching. To our colleagues in the Department of Educational Leadership at Concordia University Chicago, we say thanks for editing our drafts, encouraging us to continue, and inspiring us with new ideas. To Dr. Sandra McLendon, Dean of the School of Education at Southern Wesleyan University, thank you for your support through time, talent, and adoption of our book. To our families and friends, we are indebted to you for your willingness to sacrifice and your ever-constant support in this endeavor. Our love and gratitude are immeasurable.

Special thanks to Robert W. Olson (1938–2015) for his leadership and guidance. We are also thankful for those fellow educators who endorsed this book and whose comments led to refinement. We thank those who provided testimonies for the first edition, which are now reflected in the second edition. Kimberly Strike was the lead author of this book. We, your fellow authors, are filled with gratitude for your creativity, hard work, and dedication to completing this task. We will never forget your enthusiasm and passion for effective leadership practices and theories. Finally, we are grateful to the editorial staff and publishers at Rowman & Littlefield and excited to be able to provide a second edition of our publication.

For all that has been, thanks!

For all that will be, yes!

References

Maxwell, J., & Elmore, T. (2007). *The Maxwell leadership bible.* (2nd ed.). Nashville, TN: Maxwell Motivation, Inc.

~

Introduction

As the evaluation and supervision of teachers has evolved in the literature and the field, the evaluation and supervision of those in leadership roles has lagged in development. Those serving directly in leadership positions have an idea of what good leadership is and what the expectations are through standards such as PSEL (2015), NELP (2018), Learning Forward, or state standards from departments or offices of public instruction.

Although national and state standards serve as guidelines, those charged with supervision and evaluation of leaders have been left to create their own evaluation tools, rating scales, or methods of feedback. This practice has presented challenges, such as interrater reliability and credibility, from district to district. Lack of a common and accepted evaluation tool may even carry legal implications. For example, a district may have to keep a person in a leadership position due to a lack of evidence or a credible evaluation tool that allows for legal protections, such as due process, and time frames for improvement.

In addition, the leader may file a grievance or lawsuit if the evaluation is untimely, subjective, or not evidence based. We have witnessed and participated in the process of supervision and evaluation. We are practitioners anchored in the theories of leadership. Approached and encouraged by colleagues serving in leadership roles, we were called to demystify the evaluation process for educational leaders. Through the exploration of knowledge, skills, dispositions, and practices of leadership recognized as effective, we developed the basis for this book, hereafter referred to as *The Leadership Framework*.

Chapter 1 defines the term *effective leadership* and explains the format of the framework. Through the use of domains, components, and elements, we have categorized the underpinning knowledge, skills, dispositions, and practices. Though some may fit across domains, their placement is based on our experience and review of the literature. This chapter provides a visual of *The Leadership Framework*, with each domain outlined in Appendix A.

Chapters 2 and 3 provide the rubrics and narrative descriptors that align with each domain. Chapter 2 focuses on Domains 1 (leadership competencies) and 4 (management competencies); chapter 3 focuses on Domains 2 (professional learning and growth practices) and 3 (instructional practices). These rubrics offer all parties involved in the evaluation and supervision of leadership clear and concise language, clear expectations, and the opportunity to move from the evaluation piece to professional learning and growth. The rubrics and narrative descriptors call for professional discussions, goal setting, and evidence throughout a process of self-reflection and continual improvement.

Chapter 4 provides a historical context of educational leadership and unpacks the traits, behaviors, and responsibilities literature identifies as necessary for school leaders. This review of literature is a bridge from contextual traits, behaviors, and responsibilities to knowledge, skills, dispositions, and practices identified within the leadership framework.

Chapter 5 provides a crosswalk of the PSEL (2015) standards, the leadership framework, and theories of leadership. This comprehensive chapter demonstrates the connections between standards, theory, practice, and evaluation. Through the examination of the connections, the reader gains a deeper understanding of the underpinnings on which evaluation occurs, and it answers the questions of what, how, and why.

Chapter 6 examines the similarities and differences between leaders and managers. It provides a meeting point for specific leadership roles through the examination of job descriptions and alignment to the leadership framework. Jobs of the same title may have very different roles and responsibilities between or even within districts, or jobs with similar duties may have different titles. This chapter offers an overview of evaluation differentiation that can and must take place for accurate, meaningful, and relevant evaluation.

Chapter 7 explores the components of professional learning and growth and alignment of one's own professional goals with those of his or her school and/or district. It examines different models of professional learning. It also compares and contrasts professional learning and training to better align the needs of the leader with meaningful, relevant professional growth. This information then guides the reader to integrate the leadership framework into the design of a professional learning plan.

Chapter 8 recognizes that the processes of evaluation and supervision are different but interrelated and complementary. This chapter takes the reader through the process of self-reflection on one's strengths and areas for growth, recognizing and describing the use of the leadership framework through the lenses of supervision and evaluation. It then guides the reader to integrate the leadership framework into a design that links evaluation with a professional learning plan.

Features of This Book

The purpose of this book is twofold. First, it is succinctly written for practitioners in the field. It provides a clear, concise, and user-friendly framework. The rubrics and narratives offer clear expectations, common language, and uniform indicators for evaluation, self-reflection, and goal setting. Together, the leadership framework, rubrics, and narratives comprise a clear system as the core of the evaluation process.

Second, this book provides aspiring leaders with a user-friendly framework that lays out knowledge, skills, dispositions, and practices of effective leaders. Through clear objectives, each chapter is directly linked to leadership standards (PSEL and NELP). Clear, practical examples relate to practitioners; aspiring leaders can envision them. The topics are useful for anyone who wishes to better understand the alignment of standards, theory, practice, evaluation, and professional learning and growth.

Each chapter includes objectives (aligned with PSEL and NELP), a case study, discussion questions posed through the lens of a leader, and the opportunity for self-reflection and practice.

Other features include:

- The rationale for the need of a user-friendly evaluation process for educational leaders
- The value of self-reflection to drive goal setting
- Guidance to connect evaluation, goal setting, and professional learning and growth opportunities
- Recognition of the importance of evaluation differentiation
- A comprehensive description of the connections between standards, theory, and practice
- Common language that connects national, state, and local expectations of those serving in leadership roles

- Recognition of the process of supervision and evaluation for leaders at both the district and school levels

Organization of the Book

This book is organized so that those charged with the supervision and evaluation of leaders, those in a position of educational leadership that calls for supervision and evaluation, or those aspiring leaders have tools and common language to clarify the knowledge, skills, dispositions, and practices of effective educational leaders. Each chapter provides an instrumental piece as well as practical tools and case studies to explain the process of supervision and evaluation. Each chapter focuses on a part of the whole, and together they create a complete, comprehensive picture of effective leadership. In reading the book in its entirety, the reader connects leadership standards, leadership theories, and practices of effective leaders.

~

CHAPTER ONE

Setting the Stage for a Leadership Framework

When you talk about school improvement, you are talking about people improvement.

—Earnest Boyer (quoted in Sparks, 1984, p. 35)

Objectives

At the conclusion of this chapter you will be able to:

1. Distinguish individual and collective knowledge, skills, dispositions, and practices to promote the academic success and personal well-being of every student (PSEL 1, 3, 4, 5, 6, 7, 8, 9, 10; NELP 1, 3, 6).
2. Evaluate and support ongoing and differentiated professional learning through evidence-based data and self-assessment (PSEL 4, 5, 6, 7, 8, 9; NELP 2, 5, 6).
3. Differentiate *The Framework for Effective Leadership* as a research-anchored and valid tool of supervision and evaluation of educational leaders (PSEL 3, 6, 7; NELP 2, 3).
4. Relate the basis for ongoing, informative, and actionable feedback to educational leaders (PSEL 1, 3, 5, 6, 8, 9; NELP 2, 3, 5, 6).
5. Develop, support, and critique an effective evaluation system that develops leadership skills, promotes a culture of shared accountability,

and creates and supports a productive and trusting environment (PSEL 1, 2, 3, 4, 5, 6, 7, 10; NELP 1, 2, 3, 4, 5, 6).

Definition of Effective Leadership

In 2007, Charlotte Danielson shared her second edition of *Enhancing Professional Practice: A Framework for Teaching*, forever changing the role and evaluation of teachers. Within this work, Danielson describes effective teaching through identification of aspects of a teacher's responsibilities to promote improved student learning. The description comes down to knowledge, skills, dispositions, and practices shared by teachers who have mastered their craft.

Hattie (2009) provided a description of effective teaching, and it was not defined but described as "an act of teaching" with specific knowledge and awareness necessary to lead the learner to a new level of cognition. Marzano's (2007) evaluation of effective teaching includes the direct cause-and-effect relationship between teaching practices and student achievement and teachers making informed decisions to yield the greatest benefits for their students.

There is no doubt that "The quality of an education system cannot exceed the quality of its teachers" (Barber & Mourshed, 2007, p. 13). Kouzes and Posner's research confirmed the impact of teachers when they were second only to parents as having the greatest influence on people's lives (as cited in DuFour & Marzano, 2011, p. 3). We see how effective teaching is a complex interconnectedness of knowledge, skills, dispositions, and practices, yet the word *effective* is left undefined.

With close to a half million books on leadership available on Amazon alone, the authors have found the definition of *effective leadership* to be attached to a multitude of skills, traits, and characteristics; however, this is not always reflective of practice. Peter Economy (2013) states,

> A remarkable amount of time, effort, and money has been devoted to the study of leadership. Despite all this research, there is little agreement about exactly what leadership is.
>
> Still, people know effective leadership when they see it. And while great leaders may sometimes be born that way, there are certain traits that great leaders share in common that anyone can practice and adopt to become more effective. (para. 1, 2)

Through the work of Stephen Covey, traits of effective people have been identified and described. Others have followed with their own lists of traits of highly effective people or leaders. While the authors of the lists may use their own vocabulary to describe the traits, the underlying meanings are often the same. An example of this is Covey's identification of Habit 6 in which he uses the term *synergize*. Covey (1989) characterizes synergy as teamwork, open mindedness, and the adventure of finding new solutions to old problems. While familiar with each of the examples separately, Covey combines them to create an understanding of the term and provide new energy. "The possibilities of truly significant gain, of significant improvement are so real that it's worth the risk such openness entails" (p. 269).

While the educational sector functions differently than other areas, effective leadership is similar. We know and understand characteristics of *good* or *effective* leaders, such as working with others to achieve common goals or understanding that no one person can work in isolation and accomplish great things, no matter how smart or driven or wonderful.

An article in *Forbes* magazine captured the very meaning of *effective leadership* when the author, Glenn Llopis (2014), stated, "The best leaders know how to get the most out of people; they enable the full potential in others" (para. 1). He goes on to state, "Success as a leader is a by-product of the leaders and mentors we associate with throughout our careers" (para. 2). Llopis then goes on to describe effective leaders, as Covey or others have done, stating that effective leaders:

> Each brought a unique perspective to my development and their wisdom pushed me to see things about my own leadership capabilities and aptitudes that I had never seen, fully appreciated or understood before. . . . Every employee is different, with their own set of experiences, values, cultural backgrounds, influences and beliefs. The best leaders are those that can identify and appreciate the differences that one brings to the table and knows how to put them to full use. . . . They know how to take you out of your comfort zone to put your potential to the test. They observe your ability to stretch yourself and whether or not you accept the challenges. You know that you have found the right leader in your career when they never allow you to grow complacent and are constantly testing and helping you develop your skill-sets and capabilities to prepare you for the next phase in your career. (para. 3, 5, 6)

To define *effective*, we must examine *effective leadership* through consideration of the traits, level of knowledge and expertise, skill sets, dispositions, relational qualities, and application to daily practice. Effective leaders look in the mirror, not out a window, to make improvements. By definition then, *effective leadership* is exhibiting the passion and purpose to change, clearly communicating to stakeholders, leading and influencing others to work toward a shared vision, enabling others to thrive, and focusing on results.

Identification of Knowledge, Skills, Dispositions, and Practices

Leaders in the field of education face constant change and daunting challenges. We are called upon to raise standards through rigor and depth to bring *all* students to a new level of understanding; close achievement gaps; increase attendance and decrease truancy; increase graduation rates; increase student performance on high stakes tests; promote ongoing professional learning of all faculty and staff; develop partnerships with community and families; and shift to an evaluation system that calls for goal setting, self-assessment, reflection, and interrater reliability.

While each of these initiatives are important, educators have felt the impact of several mandatory initiatives within a short time period, and often with decreased resources. As effective leaders, we must articulate the requirements and connect the mandates to our reality—and each has its own reality. Effective leaders adjust to the culture of the school/district, are flexible when possible (there are nonnegotiables), and walk beside and support colleagues, students, and parents, reminding each one of the significance of their work. Fullan (2007) states, "Nothing is more central to reform than the selection and development of teachers and administrators. . . . [W]hat works in some situations does not mean we can get it to work in other situations" (p. 17).

Effective leaders put processes in place to promote change and then provide pressure and support to those working side by side with us toward a shared vision. As DuFour and Marzano (2011) remind us, "It means creating conditions that help people succeed" (p. 204). James Kouzes and Barry Posner (as cited in DuFour & Marzano, 2011) state:

> People said the leader made them feel empowered, listened to, understood, capable, important, like they mattered, challenged to do more. The overwhelming sense we get from thousands and thousands of these responses is that the best leaders take action that make people feel strong and capable. They make people feel they can do more than they thought they could do. (p. 204)

For leaders to help others make meaning of change requires bringing them to a level of understanding about performance based on a culture of continuous improvement. This process must begin with oneself. Tomal, Schilling, and Trybus (2013) tell us, "To help foster understanding, individuals need to realize that, in most cases, the school as an organization is driving change in order to improve, grow and meet increasing demands" (p. 3).

Rationale for *The Framework for Effective Leadership*

While chapter 5 will focus on leadership theory and chapter 6 will connect theory to standards, it is important that we understand the evolution of leadership and how leaders in education have transformed. Green (2017) defines leadership as

> a process used by leaders to give purpose to the collective efforts of members of the organization while influencing them to work collaboratively in an environment of mutual respect and trust. During this process, the leader assists individuals in understanding and adjusting to the environment of the organization and building their capacity so that their talents and contributions are fully leveraged. (p. 38)

Green's use of this definition is recognition of how leadership has evolved throughout the years. In the 1950s, Ohio State's Leadership Department identified two dimensions: initiating structure, which was *task-oriented leader behavior*, and consideration, which was *people-oriented leader behavior* (Halpin, 1957). At the same time, the University of Michigan conducted a series of studies of leadership that identified *task-oriented behavior*, *relationship-oriented behavior*, and *participative leadership behavior*. The Michigan findings added participative leadership, which looked at leading teams and not just individuals (Likert, 1961). Fiedler's contingency theory (1964) received a lot of attention because, at the time, it offered one of the best frameworks that examined one's leadership style, the organizational setting, and how that relationship affects leader effectiveness.

The Ohio State leadership studies affected Blake and Mouton's (1985) managerial grid, which identified *concern for production* (task) and *concern for people* (relationship). Additional studies used different labels for leadership behaviors examined through different lenses. But to generalize, the research shows being task oriented along with positive interpersonal skills is evident in effective leaders.

In 1971, R. J. House theorized that the behavior of leaders has an effect on the performance and satisfaction level of followers and the type of behavior displayed by the leader to motivate and bring satisfaction to followers is dependent on the situation, adding another dimension to the equation. "Such factors as the ability and personality of the followers, the characteristics of the work environment, and work group preferences contribute to the satisfaction and motivational level of followers and must be given consideration" (Green, 2017, p. 55). House's four categories of leadership behavior are shown in Table 1.1. This theory shifted leadership from a top-down managerial role to acquiring commitment from members and motivating them to work toward common goals within the organization.

Table 1.1   House's Categories of Leadership Behavior

Supportive Leadership	A supportive leader is approachable, maintains a pleasant work environment, is considerate, and shows concern for the needs and well-being of followers.
Directive Leadership	A directive leader sets performance standards, lets followers know what is expected of them, schedules the work, and establishes specific directions.
Participative Leadership	A participative leader consults with followers concerning work-related matters and takes their opinions into consideration when making decisions.
Achievement-Oriented Leadership	An achievement-oriented leader stresses excellence in performance, sets goals that are challenging, and shows confidence in the ability of followers to achieve challenging performance standards.

Source: Adapted from Green, R. L. (2017). *Practicing the art of leadership: A problem-based approach to implementing the professional standards for educational leaders*. (5th ed.). New York, NY: Pearson Education, Inc., p. 56.

Paul Hersey and Kenneth Blanchard (1982) introduced the *theory of situational leadership*, which expanded the idea of leadership by adding the variable of the level of maturity of the followers to perform the task and willingness to accept responsibility for completion. Though variables of task and relationship were still identified, the leader's engagement of explanation of the task and extent of communication required for successful completion of the task determined the leadership styles of *directing, coaching, supporting,* or *delegating*.

Contemporary leadership studies have called for us to look at additional factors, such as *power, authority, trust, respect,* and *reflection*. These traits are difficult to measure when examining accountability. When reviewing types of leadership, traits of leadership, or expectations of leaders, it is natural that a leader would demonstrate competency or a higher feeling of security in some areas over others.

Today's leaders are called to collect data (e.g., surveys, professional discussions, and seek critical input from a mentor or colleague), process that data, and create professional goals to support ongoing professional growth. Leadership is complex, and there must be a balance and demonstration of competency. *The Framework for Effective Leadership*, hereafter known as *The Leadership Framework*, is meant to assist with and guide the identification of those knowledge, skills, dispositions, and practices found in an effective and competent leader.

In *Leading School Change: Maximizing Resources for School Improvement*, Tomal et al. (2013) recommend a change framework that sets the context for change and demonstrates an interrelatedness of individual, group, and organizational needs for successful change processes. Therefore, leaders need a framework to skillfully draw from the wells of practice and theory. Leaders need a model of knowledge, skills, dispositions, and practices that mark the effective leader.

To do so, the authors studied Danielson's (2007) *Framework for Teaching*, which was created to enhance the professional practice of teaching. A conversation with Charlotte Danielson confirmed her focus on effective teaching, and she encouraged the authors to develop a framework focused on effective leadership. Various guidelines and tools created to guide effective educational leaders were explored, as was the literature around leadership frameworks.

In 2005, the Maryland State Board of Education published *Maryland Instructional Leadership Framework*. It includes elements and evidence of best practices for principals. However, it is narrowly based on instruction, not a broad overview of leadership. It is also dated.

Waters and Cameron (2007) published the *Balanced Leadership Framework* through Mid-continent Research for Education and Learning (McREL). It focused on 21 leadership responsibilities and associated practices related to effective leadership. However, it is not directly aligned to standards. It is also dated. Several states have leadership standards or models of leadership traits. However, they are not in a domain format useful for facilitating evaluations and professional growth opportunities. The authors also had conversations with area superintendents and confirmed there was a need in the field for a framework in leadership with clear and specific rubrics that can be used in supervision and evaluation of educational leaders.

Through commissioned work focused on leadership practice, such as Interstate School Leaders Licensure Consortium (ISLLC, 2015) and Educational Leadership Constituent Council (2011), key dispositions essential to successful leadership have been identified, such as *growth oriented, collaborative, innovative, analytical, ethical, perseverant, reflective,* and *equity minded* (Interstate School Leaders Licensure Consortium, 2015, p. 9). The standards can serve as a foundation for university training programs and practicing leaders in the field to help develop, support, and guide them in effective professional growth opportunities. *The Leadership Framework* is intended to assist in this effective growth process.

Through development of *The Leadership Framework*, the authors have organized and enhanced these ideas into a system that is embedded in best practices and research. In addition, *The Leadership Framework* supports professional learning for continuous growth and improvement; creates and supports the opportunity to develop, supervise, evaluate, mentor, and coach leaders; and calls for accountability.

While *The Leadership Framework* provides structure to the supervision and evaluation process, the authors understand the need for a comprehensive and relevant resource that identifies specific knowledge, skills, dispositions, and practices of effective leadership in which professional learning and growth opportunities are embedded. *The Leadership Framework* was created with a vision of a professional growth process that is practical, user friendly, and relevant. The executive director of Learning Forward, Joellen Killion (2011), reminds us:

> When educators are given permission and professional respect to inquire into their own practice, to discover what works within their unique communities, they not only solve the presenting problem, but they also refine their expertise with inquiry, problem solving, innovation, evaluation and improvement efforts. (p. 14)

Many accreditation and state certification and licensure boards are requiring training in newer models of supervision and evaluation. *The Leadership Framework* provides just that—a framework to assist in and support training for current and aspiring school and district leaders who are or will supervise and evaluate school and other district leaders.

Capturing the Complexity of Effective Leadership

This book offers one set of rubrics aligned with the PSEL (2015) and NELP (2018) standards, through which educational leaders can be supervised, evaluated, coached, mentored, provided opportunity to practice, and anchored in a model that promotes professional learning and growth. *The Leadership Framework* is helpful for aspiring administrators in leadership programs as well as administrators engaged in professional learning at the district and school level because it provides elements and alignment with standards helpful in self-reflection of personal strengths and areas in need of improvement. The four domains of *The Leadership Framework* are:

- Domain 1: *Leadership Competencies*
- Domain 2: *Professional Learning and Growth*
- Domain 3: *Instructional Practices*
- Domain 4: *Management Competencies*

The Leadership Framework captures the complexity of leadership and highlights that the skills are interrelated. While not a checklist, *The Leadership Framework* provides common traits of those in leadership positions. It offers a means through which leaders can view skills commonly identified in leadership within a context of self-assessment, reflection, identification of goals, and continuous improvement. It also promotes common language for professional dialogue and ongoing professional learning.

The Leadership Framework highlights successful, accomplished, and effective professional practice through a lens that identifies and defines what leaders should know (theory) and do (practice). It also allows us to identify inconsistent performance or areas of need due to lack of experience, expertise, or commitment. *The Leadership Framework* can be used in a formative or summative setting. It is the authors' intent to provide the framework for formative evaluation in an effort to promote ongoing professional learning and growth of our leaders.

Using *The Leadership Framework*

The Leadership Framework has two main parts: the framework and the rubrics that align with the framework. The rubrics reflect each component within the four domains and are broken down to capture the essential information of the elements within that component. The rubric reflects the variance of performance for each of the elements. For the purpose of this book, the authors have coupled Domains 2 and 3 and Domains 1 and 4. Each will be reviewed in depth in future chapters.

After reviewing the literature and exploring standards associated with leadership, the authors have structured the framework within four domains that reflect general areas of knowledge. There are 18 components identified, each describing specific skills within the domain. Each component is broken down to explicit dispositions and practices of effective leaders. There are 90 elements identified by the authors.

While *The Leadership Framework* exceeds the number of components within Danielson's (2007) *Framework for Teaching*, we must keep in mind the complex responsibilities of successful school and district leadership. Each framework (*Framework for Teaching* and *The Leadership Framework*) serves a specific purpose; therefore, each needs to align with the knowledge, skills, dispositions, and practices needed to be an effective teacher or effective leader, respectively. Appendix A provides *The Framework for Effective Leadership* in its entirety. This allows the reader to see the domains, components, and elements as a whole.

The reader sees the domains are divided into quadrants. Start at the top left, move to the top right, then lower right, and finally the bottom left to follow the domains in order of number. Within each domain you find numbered components, and under the numbered components are bulleted elements. Therefore, we move from the general knowledge category, to the subsets of skills in the components, to the elements that reflect the dispositions and practices required.

For example, Domain 3: *Instructional Practices*, contains four components and 20 elements. The second component in this domain is "Advocates for instruction that supports the needs of all learners." Under this component, the first element is "Provides teachers with data to drive instruction and the training to execute." The domain applies to all educators because we are all focused on student learning. The component, while still important to all educators, is targeted toward the expectations of the person, based on his or her role. The element conveys the disposition or practice required of the effective leader in order to support stakeholders and move the building or district forward.

It is important to note that, while domains may have a different number of components and the components a different number of elements, each domain reflects an equally important aspect of effective leadership, each element is of the same weight as other elements, and each component is of the same weight as other components. *The Leadership Framework* includes each concept only once, even though there may be some overlapping in day-to-day practices. Finally, the verbs used focus on active performance rather than beliefs, dispositions, or intentions. Actions can be observed and analyzed, and each verb was carefully chosen to align with and highlight the desired action for effective leadership. We further examine each domain of *The Leadership Framework* independently in Appendix A.

The Four Domains of *The Framework for Effective Leadership*

Talk with any person in a leadership position and he or she will confirm that leaders are pulled in many directions throughout the day. There is no job description that could capture all that leaders do, but there are identical threads that run through leadership, regardless of one's position. These areas are identified in the four domains of the Framework: *Leadership Competencies*, *Professional Learning and Growth*, *Instructional Practices*, and *Management Competencies*.

Leadership Competencies describes the foundational competencies leaders need to lead effectively. This domain represents the very infrastructure required to lead effectively and the character traits of effective leaders. These foundational components include: establishes a solid foundation; builds shared leadership; initiates effective communication; adheres to a moral compass; and promotes a positive school culture.

Professional Learning and Growth Practices describes competencies an effective leader needs in order to foster, facilitate, promote, and support continual improvement. These components include: demonstrates competence as an educational leader; fosters and facilitates continual improvement; promotes professional learning and growth; and supports school personnel.

Instructional Practices incorporates all of the must dos to provide the pressure and support teachers need to meet the requirements imposed through mandates, the district, the school, stakeholders, and other influences to elevate every student to his or her potential. These components include: champions and supports curriculum development; advocates for instruction that supports the needs of all learners; analyzes assessments; and incorporates technology to enhance learning.

Management Competencies addresses the areas required of leaders to manage the district or building. These components include: adheres to personnel requirements; reports accurately and timely; upholds rules and regulations; researches, secures, and stewards resources; and manages effectively.

The Need for Commonality

While each school exhibits a culture of its own, there is a need for commonality with regard to direction and influence as reflected in the following:

- A need for school district and school leaders to demonstrate proficiency in teacher and administrator evaluation processes that reflect interrater reliability.
- A need for educational leaders to share a common language and knowledge of effective models for personal and professional growth, alignment with national and state standards, and, most importantly, an increase in student performance.

- Importance for district and school leaders to have an understanding of the interrelatedness of supervision, evaluation, and professional learning and growth.
- Common language for professional dialogue.
- It is only through commonality in these areas that we can fully understand leadership in education and related organizations. It is commonality in language that fosters open professional dialogue about what defines educational leadership, what effective leadership looks like or doesn't look like, and how it is evaluated. Advocating for this foundational commonality provides the basis for professional discussions, discusses the challenges, and creates solutions while looking through the same lens of effective leadership.

Self-Assessment and Reflection in Leadership

The key to growth is self-assessment and reflection. We must be honest with ourselves in order to maximize our learning opportunities. Clear descriptions of expectations set the stage for personal reflection. If we are open and honest with ourselves, it is inevitable that, when we read through thorough descriptions, we ascertain where we are within the continuum. As seasoned practitioners, we have the metacognition of knowing where we are and a vision of where we want to be. Every person has areas in which to grow and continue in self-improvement. If we are not at a distinguished level, then we have a clear understanding of where we ought to envision ourselves and how we set clear goals for self-improvement.

There is another area that we must openly and honestly reflect on, and that is our relationship with others. This goes beyond our daily relationships with stakeholders (e.g., personnel, students, board members, parents, and community members). We must look at ourselves as we are perceived, not as we think we project ourselves. This may call for some critical introspection and feedback for us to fully understand. It calls for us to collect data on ourselves (e.g., surveys, professional discussions, and talk with one's mentor), process, and reflect on the feedback.

Some areas may be easily changed once we are aware of how we are performing or how we are perceived. However, other areas may be very difficult or even unchangeable due to our personality. In this case, we need to carefully examine how this trait is affecting how one functions within the organization, what can be done to strengthen relationships, or how we demonstrate commitment to the goals of the organization.

Uses of *The Leadership Framework*

Regardless of one's role or responsibilities with the school, the ultimate goal is to increase student learning. This is highlighted in ISLLC (2015):

> Today, educational leadership is a collaborative effort distributed among a number of professionals in schools and districts. District leaders hold positions such as superintendents, curriculum supervisors, talent management specialists, assessment directors, principal supervisors and professional learning providers. Their titles may vary, but they are all charged with the same fundamental challenge: Transform public schools to increase student learning and achievement. (p. 3)

The Leadership Framework can be used in several ways to support this collaborative effort, such as evaluation, supervision, mentoring, coaching, preparation of new leadership, a guide for professional learning for current leaders, a road map for novice or hopeful leaders, identification of targets for school improvement, and communication to the larger community.

Beyond the school setting, *The Leadership Framework* can inform licensure requirements and guide the preparation of aspiring educational leaders. Each of these uses calls for accountability and continued growth.

Evaluation. Though this function of *The Leadership Framework* is important, the authors believe evaluation is part of a cyclical process that includes goal setting, supervision, reflection, coaching, professional discussion, and specific feedback. *The Leadership Framework* can be used for evaluative purposes, both in formative and summative nature.

As a formative tool, *The Leadership Framework* provides structured and categorized knowledge, skills, dispositions, and practices. The leader has knowledge of expectations, with clear indicators. The rubrics provide specific vocabulary that defines the level of functioning. The leader must be a reflective practitioner and honestly and accurately place himself or herself within the rubric. This allows the leader to use the tool to set goals and increase level of performance through a focused practice in targeted areas.

When used as a summative tool, ongoing communication with the evaluator and evidence of each indicator create a picture of one's leadership. As with any summative tool, it is important to obtain data from multiple data points; therefore, the ongoing communication and evidence provide the leader the opportunity to demonstrate leadership capabilities and successes across time. It is highly encouraged that *The Leadership Framework* not only be used for evaluation purposes in and of itself but also as part of a process that includes coaching and professional learning and growth.

As part of the ongoing cycle, a leader should actively engage in self-evaluation, reflection, and goal setting followed by formal evaluation, specific feedback, and goal setting reflective of the feedback from the formal evaluation and goals of the organization. *The Leadership Framework* provides clear, articulate expectations, through which a district leader can evaluate school leaders accordingly. As stated by Sergiovanni and Green (as cited in Green, 2017),

> a critical factor identified in the works of the above mentioned researchers and writers is an assessment of human achievement. For the assessment to be conducted fairly and effectively and for the moral imperative to be actualized, standards of performance need to be established and met. For example, a school leader may have a vision for the school, but the questions posed are whether the leader's vision is adequate and whether the approach used to communicate that vision to all stakeholders is appropriate and effective. (p. 8)

Supervision and evaluation can be challenging for superintendents or any district leader charged with evaluating and supervising other leaders. Creating an ongoing and effective supervision and evaluation process is necessary to the climate and health of the district and the schools. *The Leadership Framework* can be used as a tool to guide this process. It helps to set the stage for ongoing mentoring, coaching, and formal evaluations required by boards of education and also for employment decisions. The use of *The Leadership Framework* for this important area will be addressed in more depth in chapter 7.

Mentoring. This step is often skipped at the leadership level. It's assumed that, once you obtain a leadership position at the district or building level, you will be self-sufficient to figure things out on your own and resourceful enough to obtain the assistance you need to succeed. While we see the benefits of mentoring teachers and increasing retention if teachers are properly oriented, trained, and supported, the isolation of building or district leaders creates a barrier few districts have sought to overcome.

Knowing and understanding expectations provides a foundation on which those new to leadership positions can build. Providing *The Leadership Framework* takes out the guesswork of what is supposed to be done and provides a level of understanding to the process. Just as teachers are provided time to acclimate and grow in their positions, so must leaders.

Coaching. Leaders need a professional network that they can trust will be confidential. Leaders have questions but may believe that they can't go to their superior or they will be viewed as incompetent or less than capable.

Some leaders are geographically or systemically separated from other leaders, so they find it difficult to talk to their peers about challenges or problems they are facing.

Coaching is productive because it provides a safe place to openly discuss challenges or miscues within a nonevaluative and nonjudgmental setting and offers the opportunity to celebrate successes. It provides a safe place to exchange ideas and the opportunity to receive feedback to provide direction and growth. *The Leadership Framework* provides specific knowledge, skills, dispositions, and practices from which the leader or the coach can identify areas of focus for practice or improvement.

Preparation of new leadership. Regardless of the size of the district or school, there are opportunities to build leaders from within. It is inevitable that there are faculty or staff members who display leadership skills or dispositions. There needs to be dialogue with them about their aspirations. *The Leadership Framework* provides the perfect guide to inform current leaders in recruiting and cultivating prospective leaders.

Professional learning and growth. When developing professional learning opportunities for staff, considerations must be made regarding current initiatives, needs of the school, interests of the staff, and training or professional learning needs of the staff; in other words, what does that individual need to be successful in his or her current setting and role? Leaders need the same considerations. *The Leadership Framework* is a guide for professional learning for current leaders in that it lays out the knowledge, skills, dispositions, and practices of effective leaders. As reflective practitioners, this guide is used to target areas of need or interest of further development.

Road map. Novice or aspiring leaders often do not have a level of understanding of what effective leadership looks like, nor do they know the questions to ask. It's difficult to formulate meaningful questions on a topic you don't really understand. Therefore, *The Leadership Framework* provides a road map for novice or aspiring leaders in that it lays out what effective leadership looks like as well as providing specific knowledge, skills, dispositions, and practices from which the novice can choose to focus to practice and obtain experience.

School improvement. Education has evolved into a field where its leaders are accountable for providing evidence of effective district or school leadership as indicated by students' readiness for college, careers, and life. Public perception of preparation of such skills for students is filtered from the leader, through the teachers and into the students; therefore, student success is directly linked to effective leadership. School improvement has evolved from policies and procedures to accountability for the academic success and well-being of every student. Therefore, if improvements are needed in the school, there is a call for leadership to be responsive. *The Leadership Framework* provides specific knowledge, skills, dispositions, and practices that can directly be linked to mission, vision, values, and goals of the district or school.

Communication. The *Leadership Framework* provides the benefit of common language. Whether speaking to a board member, community member, or parent, the same terminology is used. Educational jargon has been removed to reveal practical, real-life knowledge, skills, dispositions, and practices that can be understood by and communicated to the community at large.

Licensure and preparation. The *Leadership Framework* provides clear, articulate expectations of leaders. Candidates in preparatory programs for leadership or seeking licensure, certification, or endorsement are shaped by the use of *The Leadership Framework.* Through familiarity, active interaction with, and reflection on *The Leadership Framework,* candidates practice skills and behaviors directly aligned with standards where they are required to demonstrate proficiency to obtain licensure (certification or endorsement).

Summary

As the field of education has evolved, so has the need for effective leadership. The identification of standards through commissions, such as PSEL and NELP, clarify the important work and responsibilities of learning-focused leaders. *The Leadership Framework* organizes the knowledge, skills, dispositions, and practices of effective leaders into a practical, relevant, user-friendly guide. *The Leadership Framework* provides common language and rubrics for interreliability in the supervision and evaluation process. It provides a common level of terminology for better understanding by stakeholders, and a common language for profession discussions and dialogue.

The Leadership Framework can be used in a variety of ways, including evaluation, supervision, mentoring, coaching, preparation of new leadership, a guide for professional learning for current leaders, a road map for novice or hopeful leaders, identification of targets for school improvement, communication to the larger community, preparatory programs for leadership, and licensure preparation.

Chapter 2 and chapter 3 will examine the collective characteristics of effective leaders through the lens of rubrics and narrative descriptors.

Self-Assessment and Reflection

Please refer to *The Leadership Framework* (Appendix A). As you read through *The Leadership Framework* a second time, ask yourself these questions in relation to your own strengths and weaknesses:

1. Which of the domains stands out to you as an area of strength?
2. With which components and elements within the domain do you best associate?
3. Which components do you think might challenge you the most or that you avoid? Acknowledging these areas as challenging, what could you do to foster success in these specific areas?
4. Are there elements listed that you view as challenging due to environmental circumstances associated with your specific placement or position?
5. How do you envision *The Leadership Framework* as a tool for you to use to expand your personal learning and professional growth?
6. How would you differentiate the use of *The Leadership Framework* with colleagues, subordinates, or superiors?
7. How will you demonstrate growth in identified areas?
8. What evidence would you have to substantiate your claims?

References

Barber, M., & Mourshed, M. (2007, September). How the world's best-performing school systems come out on top. *McKinsey & Company*. Retrieved from https://www.mckinsey.com/~/media/McKinsey/Industries/Social%20Sector/Our%20Insights/How%20the%20worlds%20best%20performing%20school%20systems%20come%20out%20on%20top/How_the_world_s_best-performing_school_systems_come_out_on_top.ashx

Blake, R. R., & Mouton, J. S. (1985). *The managerial grid III*. Houston, TX: Gulf Publishing Company.

Covey, S. R. (1989). *The seven habits of highly effective people: Restoring the character ethic*. New York, NY: Simon & Schuster.

Danielson, C. (2007). *Enhancing professional practice: A framework for teaching*. Alexandria, VA: Association for Supervision and Curriculum Development.

DuFour, R., & Marzano, R. (2011). *Leaders of learning: How district, school, and classroom leaders improve student achievement*. Bloomington, IN: Solution Tree Press.

Economy, P. (2013, August 27). 7 Traits of highly effective leaders: If you want to up your leadership game, adopt these seven qualities. *Inc*. Retrieved from http://www.inc.com/peter-economy/7-traits-highly-effective-leaders.html

Fiedler, F. E. (1964). A contingency model of leadership effectiveness. *Advances in Experimental Social Psychology, 1,* 149–190.

Fullan, M. (2007). *The new meaning of educational change.* (4th ed.). New York, NY: Teachers College Press.

Green, R. L. (2017). *Practicing the art of leadership: A problem-based approach to implementing the professional standards for educational leaders.* (5th ed.). New York, NY: Pearson Education, Inc.

Halpin, A. (1957). *Leader behavior description questionnaire.* Columbus, OH: Ohio State University, Fisher College of Business.

Hattie, J. (2009). *Visible learning: A synthesis of over 800 meta-analyses relating to student achievement.* New York, NY: Routledge.

Hersey, P., & Blanchard, K. H. (1982). *Management of organizational behavior: Utilizing human resources.* (4th ed.). Englewood Cliffs, NJ: Prentice Hall.

Interstate School Leaders Licensure Consortium. (2015). *Educational leadership policy standards: ISLLC 2015.* Washington, DC: Council of Chief State School Officers.

Killion, J. (2011, June). A bold move forward. *The Learning Professional, 32*(3), 10–14.

Likert, R. (1961). *New patterns of management.* New York, NY: McGraw-Hill.

Llopis, G. (2014, July 29). Leadership is about enabling the full potential in others. *Forbes.* Retrieved from https://www.forbes.com/sites/glennllopis/2014/07/29/leadership-is-about-enabling-the-full-potential-in-others/#146309336698

Maryland State Board of Education. (2005). *Maryland instructional leadership framework.* Retrieved from https://marylandlearninglinks.org/wp-content/uploads/2016/03/MD-Instructional-leadership-framework.pdf

Marzano, R. (2007). *The art and science of teaching: A comprehensive framework for effective instruction.* Alexandria, VA: Association for Supervision and Curriculum Development.

National Policy Board for Educational Administration. (2015). *Professional standards for educational leaders 2015.* Retrieved from http://npbea.org/wp-content/uploads/2017/06/Professional-Standards-for-Educational-Leaders_2015.pdf

National Policy Board for Educational Administration. (2018). *National educational leadership preparation (NELP) program standards: Building level.* Retrieved from http://npbea.org/wp-content/uploads/2018/11/NELP-Building-Standards.pdf

Sparks, D. (1984). Staff development and school improvement: An interview with Ernest Boyer. *Journal of Staff Development, 5*(2), 32–39.

Tomal, D., Schilling, C., & Trybus, M. (2013). *Leading school change: Maximizing resources for school improvement.* Lanham, MD: Rowman & Littlefield Publishers, Inc.

Waters, T., & Cameron, G. (2007). *The balanced leadership framework: Connecting vision with action.* Denver, CO: Mid-continent Research for Education and Learning (McREL).

CHAPTER TWO

~

The Framework for Effective Leadership

Domains 2 and 3

Your life journey is a continuing opportunity to deepen your faith, develop your gifts, and enhance your contribution to what the world becomes.

—Bolman & Deal (2001, p. 236)

Objectives

At the conclusion of this chapter you will be able to:

1. Create a comprehensive, rigorous, and coherent curricular program; develop the instructional and leadership capacity of staff; and supervise instruction (PSEL 4, 5, 6, 7; NELP 4, 5, 7, 8).
2. Ensure that teacher and organizational time is focused and protected to support high-quality instruction and student learning (PSEL 4, 5, 6, 7; NELP 3, 4).
3. Analyze assessment and accountability systems to advocate for all learners; identify and address gaps between levels of expectation and student performance; and monitor and evaluate the impact of the instructional program (PSEL 4, 5, 6, 7, 10; NELP 3, 7).
4. Promote the effective use of appropriate technologies to enhance and support teaching and learning (PSEL 3, 5, 6, 7, 8, 10; NELP 3, 4, 5, 6, 7).

Expectations and Introspection—Domains 2 and 3

This chapter examines the collective characteristics of effective leaders through the lens of the rubrics and narrative descriptors found in *The Leadership Framework*. The indicators within each rubric reflect the leadership standards of PSEL (2015), NELP (2018), and Learning Forward. A crosswalk of the standards and *The Leadership Framework* appears in chapter 5.

The framework reflects knowledge, skills, dispositions, and practices required of those in leadership positions, specifically those serving as superintendent, assistant superintendent, principal, assistant principal, department or division chair, director or coordinator, or other related leadership roles. Leadership emphasizes processes and achieves shared vision and objectives, motivates, influences, coordinates, innovates, manages, accomplishes—and changes. Yukl and Gardner (2020) state:

> The distinction between leader and follower roles does not mean that a person cannot perform both roles at the same time. . . . [V]arious leadership functions may be carried out by different people who influence what the group does, how it is done, and the way people in the group relate to each other. Leadership may be exhibited both by formally selected leaders and by informal leaders. (pp. 3–4)

Internal decisions within the district determine the terminology used to describe a role as well as the responsibilities assigned to it. In using the framework, keep in mind that informal leadership should be recognized and grown. Effective application of the framework is demonstrated in chapter 6, and chapter 8 demonstrates effective application of the framework to develop a professional learning plan.

The Framework Design

Although it is common in the literature to identify leadership characteristics and traits, less is written about the development or growth of leadership skills or evaluation of such skills. Contemporary theories and models of leadership abound, each with its own assumptions and implications. Many state departments of education offer state standards or a list of necessary knowledge, skills, dispositions, and practices identified for teachers, administrators, and counselors. While the leadership model under which the district or individual operates determines the approach to leadership and management, research is lacking in the area of evaluation of educators serving in leadership roles.

Practitioners in the field need an evaluation tool that identifies characteristics of effective leaders while concurrently providing a framework and context for the evaluation of school and district leaders. The essential notion of a framework, first, structures the work of developing an understanding for recognition of and evaluation of characteristics of effective leaders; second, provides continuity in the identification of these characteristics; and, third, offers a platform for interrater reliability. Therefore, the objective of the framework is to provide a common resource reflecting common language based on standards of practice.

Within each domain of the framework, a rubric identifies each component, defines each element in depth as an indicator for assessment purposes, and provides precise language that substantiates the requirements for that specific area. Both the person being evaluated (self-assessment, reflection, and goal setting) and the evaluator (observation, formal evaluation, specific feedback, and goal setting) should use the rubrics as part of an ongoing cycle.

To aid both the person evaluated and the evaluator, narrative descriptors are provided. The descriptors unpack and define each indicator and establish further understanding of expectations. Through common language and user-friendly explanations, the narrative descriptors provide the specifics of each element. This transparency encourages self-reflection, identification of areas of strength and need, the ability to target one's current and desired levels of performance, and guidance to set professional goals.

The Leadership Framework promotes continued improvement, both personal and professional. Evaluation is an active process through which the person evaluated knows the expectations (application); is provided descriptive narrative and specific, timely feedback (commendation and recommendation); is provided time to discern (reflection and self-assessment); develops a plan; and engages in the cyclical process for ongoing learning and improvement.

The person evaluated has the opportunity to see the rubric prior to the evaluation process and place himself or herself within the context of the rubric with justification and evidence of that placement. The evaluator also has the opportunity to place the person evaluated in the rubric with justification and evidence. The two have a professional conversation based on placement on the rubrics. Professional goals are established based on the placement, with a plan to monitor, provide evidence of progress, and reevaluate.

The professional conversation should take place in a timely manner, identify two or three specific elements as areas of focus for a single observation or professional discussion, and be initiated by the person being evaluated to obtain reflective thoughts, first, and then discuss alignment to the rubric.

Trust is imperative. The conversation must take place in a comfortable, safe environment, and the process needs to be highly reflective. Danielson (2007) shares John Dewey's conclusion that "we learn not from our experience but from our thinking *about* that experience. It is the *thinking* that matters" (p. 169). Providing a safe environment promotes honest, accurate reflection and a focus on growth.

Following this alignment and reflection, the evaluator can then provide meaningful feedback. Together, they should identify future areas of focus that reflect interest, areas in need of further development, or strengths with further elaboration and growth. With input from both, two or three professional goals are developed, and the cyclical process continues.

In partnership, the evaluator teaches the power of reflection and assists with the development of skills needed to become an effective leader. Through a systematic, analytic reflection, skills are developed to accurately recognize what has gone well and what hasn't. Internalization coupled with professional conversation provides the opportunity to develop goals to improve these areas and evidence that confirms targeted outcomes have been met. It is important to focus professional learning and growth to meet the needs of the individual.

A novice leader does not need a separate framework because all leaders need to exemplify the same skills. The experienced leader should demonstrate skills at an advanced level and with automaticity. Therefore, experienced leaders are not called to complete greater tasks but, rather, to demonstrate a deeper level of understanding or greater skill to complete tasks successfully. *The Leadership Framework* accounts for varying levels of experience and skills of the person being evaluated. It provides the evaluator a user-friendly resource to make informed decisions about knowledge, skills, dispositions, and practices evident in effective leaders.

Rubrics

Providing the rubrics to the person being evaluated at the very beginning of the process demonstrates open communication; establishes a baseline for trust; extinguishes the thought of a gotcha system; promotes self-reflection to establish goals; promotes common language for professional conversations; articulates clear expectations; enhances the quality of work; establishes a sense of purpose; and creates the structure for a defined, structured evaluation process.

To organize an interrelated process, the framework categorizes the knowledge, skills, dispositions, and practices of effective leaders into four domains. Each heading (component) listed within the domain identifies the skills of effective leaders and provides detailed dispositions and practices (elements) as specific examples. Each component is the focus of a separate rubric with the elements serving as indicators. Each indicator is placed within four levels of performance: *Unsatisfactory, Basic, Proficient,* and *Distinguished.*

According to Foley, Mishook, Thompson, Kubiak, Supovitz, and Rhude-Faust (2008), an indicator becomes a *leading indicator* when it is timely and accurate as described below:

Indicator—reported with enough time to change a course of action.

Benchmarked—users understand what constitutes improvement in a leading indicator through connection of metrics.

Powerful—it offers targets for improvement in a leading indicator and shows progress, or lack of progress, toward a desired outcome before that outcome occurs. (p. 3)

The following section describes the rubrics and their use related to Domains 2 and 3. These domains focus on knowledge, skills, dispositions, and practices of leaders as they relate to *Professional Learning and Growth Practice* and *Instructional Practices.* An effective leader must keep current on mandates, major initiatives, research, and trends. In addition to creating opportunities for leaders' learning and identification of growth goals, it is important to foster opportunities and provide support for staff to establish and meet individual needs for professional learning and growth.

Levels of Performance

Experienced and effective school leaders hone their leadership skills and expertise over time through ongoing professional learning, reflective practice, constructive feedback, and effective supervision. It is imperative that the school leader strive for a high level of expertise within the arena of complex work. Experience is not the same as expertise. Amount of time on the job does not automatically equate to improvement of leadership ability, effectiveness, or success.

Within *The Leadership Framework* rubric, the identifiers of *levels of performance* are consistent throughout all domains. The ratings (unsatisfactory, basic, proficient, and distinguished) identify the levels of performance of the leader at that moment in time. This is significant because it reflects the variability of performance and patterns of behavior and assists in identifying areas of strengths as well as areas that may need improvement or more experience. Most importantly, the levels of performance should be used as a tool for supervision and evaluation as well as a platform for professional conversation and critical, specific feedback.

Unsatisfactory. A leader performing at the unsatisfactory level does not yet demonstrate evidence of the basic leadership understandings and skills associated with that component. An unsatisfactory level can stem from a multitude of reasons, including but not limited to:

- little to no understanding
- lack of prerequisite knowledge
- level of error or lack of correction of error
- lack of awareness, responsiveness, or experience
- does not indicate movement to expand one's professional skill set

Professional conversation and the development of specific professional learning goals would be expected to occur and be implemented in order for the leader to provide evidence of positive growth in the future. Professional conversation is also imperative to explore the core reasons for an unsatisfactory rating. It is the responsibility of the evaluator or supervisor to guide the plan for improvement with the leader. Specific time lines and evidence of growth within the plan are essential.

Basic. A leader performing at the basic level appears to understand the elements of the competent leader but demonstrates inconsistent implementation and application of the skills or knowledge. Leadership at the basic level is often noted in a novice leader who is encountering some of the leadership experiences for the first time. It is commonly due to lack of experience that the implementation is at the basic level.

The evaluator or supervisor of a leader at the basic level is encouraged to implement a coaching or mentoring model to achieve positive results of professional growth. Working with the leader in a supportive yet focused environment will provide the foundation for enhanced performance and improved leadership skills and dispositions.

Proficient. The leader performing at the proficient level has a solid understanding of the elements of the competent leader and demonstrates the ability to articulate and execute the appropriate leadership skills and interactions consistently with a high level of success. This level of competency is noted by others in the organization. The proficient leader has the capacity and skills to change course and move seamlessly to an alternate implementation plan if necessary.

Leaders at the proficient level work continually to improve their practice and may act as mentors to others in their professional community. The evaluator or supervisor of a proficient leader is encouraged to be supportive of the efforts of the leader and provide an appropriate platform for continued growth and success.

Distinguished. The leader performing at the distinguished level is a master of the craft. The distinguished leader consistently performs at the highest level and prominent success. This level of leadership is qualitatively and quantitatively different from those of their colleagues. The distinguished leader is a contributor to the school, community, and professional community.

Obtaining a distinguished level of performance is an admirable, attainable goal yet does not warrant a permanent rating. It is more realistic to move in and out of distinguished and proficient as the leadership role shifts and the leader continues to grow. It is also possible to not achieve a distinguished rating in all elements at the same time. The evaluator or supervisor of a distinguished leader is encouraged to be a champion of the leader's efforts and accomplishments.

Narrative Descriptors

In addition to the identification of indicators, narrative descriptions are provided for each indicator. Descriptors are important because they provide thoughtful and reflective explanations that enhance the value of the activity; make actions more thoughtful, purposeful, and rewarding; ensure high quality; and establish the foundation for deeper and more productive professional conversations. In an effort to maximize professional learning and growth, a narrative description of each component clarifies the rationale and reflects the level of skill that demonstrates effective leadership. The narrative descriptors are not meant to be comprehensive in nature but, rather, provide specific examples of behaviors often exhibited in effective leaders.

Domain 2—*Professional Learning and Growth Practices*

Domain 2 focuses on characteristics of strong, effective educational leaders. These characteristics reflect one's ability to develop one's own skills but, just as important, to develop skills and build capacity in others. This is done through shared leadership, recognizing gifts and talents, and surrendering to the good of the group rather than one's personal successes or recognition.

Leaders who are focused on the success of all are not focused on their title, wages, or vacation time but on personal relationships that reveal dreams and goals, promote and encourage, transfer knowledge, dedicate resources, and provide opportunities for growth and development.

Component 2a—Demonstrates Competence as an Educational Leader

Rationale and Explanation

Leaders lead by example, such as active engagement in events and trainings, serving as a role model, and high expectations for self and others. As instructional leaders, it's imperative to remain current in the field and continue to learn. Stagnant and outdated information will not keep up with the needs of the district, school, or students. Other areas to lead by example include ethical and moral decision-making, accountability, and responsibility. When mistakes are made, being honest, forthright, and accepting responsibility shows a person's integrity and is a window into his or her character. It is in the best interest of the district, school, and students to retain quality staff.

Providing initial support through orientation, training, and mentoring is essential. As educators progress in their knowledge and experience, coaching provides the opportunity to move to the next level. As part of a process, coaching is not a negative experience or judgmental, and negative connotations should not be attached to it. This is an opportunity to grow in one's craft.

Relationships are imperative to effective leadership, and they rely heavily on outside sources, such as boards, businesses, colleges, organizations, foundations, and other community partnerships. Such partnerships play a large part in schools through referendums, financial support or sponsorships, tours, scholarships, and special activities or events.

Demonstration

Effective leaders commit to coursework, conferences, workshops, and trainings to keep abreast in their field. When attending sessions, they model engaged participation and expected behavior, such as on-time (or early) arrival, attendance that spans the entire session, and minimal or total elimination of the use of technology for personal purposes during the session.

Component 2b—Fosters and Facilitates Continual Improvement

Rationale and Explanation

Whether a district or school is considered to be high functioning or in continuous improvement status, it's important to continually monitor, evaluate,

Table 2.1. Component 2a: Demonstrates competence as an educational leader

Element	Unsatisfactory	Basic	Proficient	Distinguished
			Level of Performance	
Researches new concepts and effectively incorporates ideas in the district	The leader fails to research best practices that may impact the school and district.	The leader inconsistently researches and applies concepts that may impact the school and district.	The leader consistently researches and effectively applies concepts with impact on the school and district.	The leader models and effectively applies concepts with impact on the school and district.
Actively participates in professional learning and growth	The leader fails to participate in professional learning and growth activities.	The leader inconsistently participates in professional learning and growth activities.	The leader actively participates in professional learning and growth activities.	The leader is an active participant in and models the implementation of professional learning and growth activities.
Provides mentoring and coaching opportunities	The leader fails to promote mentoring or coaching opportunities.	The leader inconsistently provides mentoring and coaching opportunities.	The leader provides well-defined mentoring and coaching opportunities.	The leader provides extensive and ongoing mentoring and coaching opportunities that include follow-up, collaboration, and reflection.
Models accountability and responsibility	The leader fails to model accountability and responsibility.	The leader inconsistently models accountability and responsibility.	The leader consistently models accountability and responsibility.	The leader is an exemplary model of accountability and responsibility.
Differentiates interactions with boards and organizations	The leader fails to differentiate interactions with boards and organizations.	The leader inconsistently differentiates interactions with boards and organizations.	The leader consistently demonstrates differentiated interactions with boards and organizations.	The leader always models differentiated interactions with boards and organizations.

©Strike (2016).

Table 2.2. Component 2b: Fosters and facilitates continual improvement

Level of Performance

Element	Unsatisfactory	Basic	Proficient	Distinguished
Identifies areas of discourse	The leader fails to identify areas of discourse or does not respond accordingly.	The leader inconsistently identifies areas of discourse.	The leader identifies areas of discourse.	The leader models, identifies, responds, and creates a plan of action so that areas of discourse can be eliminated or minimized.
Identifies target area/s and evaluates strategies for growth	The leader fails to identify target areas and evaluate strategies for growth.	The leader inconsistently addresses target areas and/or rarely evaluates strategies for growth.	The leader addresses target areas and evaluates strategies for growth.	The leader models, identifies target areas, and effectively evaluates strategies for growth.
Monitors progress of instruction and evaluates student learning	The leader fails to monitor progress of instruction or evaluate student learning.	The leader inconsistently monitors progress of instruction and/or evaluates student learning.	The leader monitors progress of instruction and evaluates student learning.	The leader always monitors progress of instruction and evaluates student learning.
Evaluates programs and processes on a regular basis	The leader fails to evaluate programs and processes on a regular basis.	The leader inconsistently evaluates programs and processes on a regular basis.	The leader evaluates programs and processes on a regular basis.	The leader always evaluates programs and processes in regard to school improvement.

©Strike (2016).

and modify the school improvement and instructional learning plans. When identifying areas of professional dialogue, we first analyze, then investigate, and then put a plan in place for improvement. This process is recognized by Jim Knight in *The Impact Cycle* (2018) as identify, learn, and improve. To further advance, change is imperative to monitor, evaluate, and modify through a continuous improvement process for all stakeholders.

Demonstration
Student needs, the needs of the community, and changes in the field make it necessary continually to evaluate and make improvements. Continual improvement calls for us to celebrate successes and offer accolades to those who participate in the success, understand a work in progress, and embrace continual improvement as an ongoing project.

Component 2c—Promotes Professional Learning and Growth

Rationale and Explanation
Effective leaders provide opportunities for training and professional learning that align with district, school, and professional mission, vision, and goals. Coupled with clear communication, these opportunities provide a level of comfort because they ensure that proper training takes place so stakeholders have a firm understanding of initiatives, policies, and procedures. Using walk-throughs, pop-ins, and observations, leaders can work with staff to identify areas of need and interest specific to the individual teacher, classroom, and groups of students.

Professional learning and growth must be relevant to the needs and roles of the participants. When preparing professional learning opportunities, it is essential to obtain input from participants to identify areas of need and interest. Other areas for consideration in planning effective professional learning are scheduling; building on existing knowledge and skills; length, depth, and amount of material; effective communication; selection and adaptation of the environment; and celebrating accomplishments.

Effective leaders find the resources to fund ongoing professional growth and support dissemination of knowledge. Professional learning and growth sessions are opportune times to share gifts and talents within the district or between neighboring districts. Sharing resources provides greater opportunities to tap into local professional talent as well as bring in outside presenters who may be too expensive for one district.

Table 2.3. Component 2c: Promotes professional learning and growth

	Level of Performance			
Element	Unsatisfactory	Basic	Proficient	Distinguished
Ensures appropriate timing, time frame, and fiscal commitment	The leader fails to provide fiscal commitment or effective timing for professional growth.	The leader inconsistently provides appropriate timing, time frame, and fiscal commitment.	The leader provides appropriate timing, time frame, and fiscal commitment.	The leader always ensures appropriate timing, time frame, and fiscal commitment.
Provides opportunities for professional learning both in and out of district	The leader fails to provide opportunities for professional learning.	The leader inconsistently provides opportunities for professional learning.	The leader provides opportunities for professional learning.	The leader always encourages and supports targeted professional learning opportunities.
Uses gifts and talents of district/school staff to peer train	The leader fails to use the gifts and talents of staff to peer train.	The leader inconsistently uses the gifts and talents of staff to peer train.	The leader uses the gifts and talents of staff to peer train.	The leader always maximizes the gifts and talents of staff to peer train.
Aligns to individual and school/district goals	The leader fails to align professional development to individual and school/district goals.	The leader inconsistently aligns professional development to individual and school/district goals.	The leader aligns professional development to individual and school/district goals.	The leader always aligns professional development to individual and school/district goals.
Ensures that participants articulate, document, and reflect on goals	The leader fails to ensure that participants can articulate, document, and reflect on goals.	The leader inconsistently ensures that participants articulate, document, and reflect on goals.	The leader ensures that participants of professional development articulate, document, and reflect on their goals.	The leader requires that participants of professional development articulate, document, and reflect on their goals.
Encourages collaborative, ongoing work resulting in positive change	The leader does not encourage collaboration or ongoing commitment that leads to positive change.	The leader inconsistently encourages collaboration and ongoing commitment to professional development that results in positive change.	The leader encourages, collaborates, and is committed to professional development that results in positive change.	The leader always models and encourages collaboration and ongoing commitment to professional development that results in positive change.
Models lifelong learning and skill acquisition	The leader fails to model lifelong learning and skill acquisition.	The leader inconsistently models lifelong learning and skill acquisition.	The leader models lifelong learning and skill acquisition.	The leader consistently models and seeks opportunities to enhance lifelong learning and skill acquisition.

©Strike (2016).

Demonstration

Effective leaders plan well in advance and identify dates for professional learning as part of the school calendar. Specific information is shared with faculty and staff multiple times and through multiple channels in order for teachers to plan for the day physically (e.g., materials and data review) as well as mentally. By providing participants with the title and description of the sessions, location for sessions and breakouts, time frame for each session, and a list of required attendees, participants know the expectations for the day. As professionals, these days should not be days on which appointments are made (e.g., doctor and dentist) or personal time taken.

Component 2d—Supports School Personnel

Rationale and Explanation

Retention of quality staff relies heavily on support of the leadership. Support starts with knowledge and understanding of content and instructional strategies. There must be an underlying knowledge and understanding to supervise effectively, particularly if serving as an evaluator. In working with staff, a relationship of trust and respect must be built. By knowing your staff members, you can better meet their needs professionally. As your relationship deepens, you can better support staff members as they experience professional highs and lows, health or personal issues.

A common complaint from teachers is that students who are sent to the office are returned to the classroom quickly and without documentation that communicates how the referral was handled. As leaders, we must provide support, follow-through, and clear communication about how the situation was handled. Following the school-wide discipline plan in place provides consistency for staff, students, and parents; however, communication must still follow. For example, the teacher in a school using PBIS who sent a student to the office with a referral needs to know the next steps taken and where the child is on the discipline matrix.

Younger students are traditionally in self-contained classrooms and may have interactions with other teachers, such as specialists, interventionists, special education teachers, or teachers who switch for RtI leveled or personalized instruction. Other areas where students may receive infractions include the cafeteria, hallway, or school transportation. Older students traditionally have several teachers throughout the day with little to no communication between them as well as other infraction areas, such as the cafeteria, hallway, or restroom. Therefore, it is important for leaders to follow through and communicate effectively with school personnel.

Table 2.4. Component 2d: Supports school personnel

Level of Performance

Element	Unsatisfactory	Basic	Proficient	Distinguished
Demonstrates understanding of content and various instructional strategies	The leader fails to demonstrate understanding of content and various instructional strategies.	The leader rarely demonstrates understanding of content and various instructional strategies.	The leader usually demonstrates a competent level of understanding of content and various instructional strategies.	The leader always demonstrates complete understanding of content and various instructional strategies with positive impact on student achievement.
Provides follow-through with discipline referrals in accordance with district/school policies	The leader does not provide follow-through with discipline referrals in accordance with district/school policies.	The leader inconsistently provides follow-through with discipline referrals in accordance with district/school policies.	The leader provides follow-through with discipline referrals in accordance with district/school policies.	The leader always provides follow-through with discipline referrals in accordance with district/school policies and works to establish an action plan for reduction of discipline referrals.
Protects instructional time	The leader fails to ensure that teacher and organizational time is focused to support quality maximization of time spent on instruction and student learning.	The leader inconsistently ensures that teacher and organizational time is focused to support maximization of time spent on quality instruction and student learning.	The leader ensures that teacher and organizational time is focused to support maximization of time spent on quality instruction and student learning.	The leader always ensures that teacher and organizational time is focused to support maximization of time spent on quality instruction and student learning.
Fosters climate that supports high expectations	The leader lacks understanding or sustenance of a school culture and instructional program conducive to student learning and does not demonstrate high expectations for all students.	The leader inconsistently demonstrates understanding; does not sustain a school culture and instructional program conducive to student learning; or does not demonstrate high expectations for all students.	The leader understands and sustains a school culture and instructional program conducive to student learning, with high expectations for all students.	The leader always demonstrates that he understands and sustains a school culture and instructional program conducive to student learning, with high expectations for all students.
Provides resources, time, roles, and structure imperative to sound instruction	The leader neither demonstrates an understanding of nor efficiently uses human, fiscal, and technical resources to support and enhance sound instruction.	The leader inconsistently demonstrates that he understands and efficiently uses human, fiscal, and technical resources to support and enhance sound instruction.	The leader demonstrates that he understands and efficiently uses human, fiscal and technical resources to support and enhance sound instruction.	The leader always demonstrates that he understands and efficiently uses human, fiscal, and technical resources to support and enhance sound instruction.

©Strike (2016).

An effective educational leader is a watchdog over instructional time. This includes setting and adhering to guidelines or rules that outline use of intercoms, phone calls to classrooms, use of cell phones by teachers/staff, monitoring of media and technology, or something as important to students and teachers as having classroom parties.

An effective leader establishes and fosters a culture that supports high expectations and provides the resources (e.g., materials, time, personnel, and structure) that are imperative to promote quality instruction. The culture of the school is based on the values and beliefs of those within and establishes how things are done and whether improvement is possible (Gruenert & Whitaker, 2015, p. 10). The climate of the school is much easier for the leader to have an effect on because it projects the group's attitude, perceptions, how people feel, and improves with positive change.

Demonstration

This area of effective leadership is the ability to connect, support, and communicate with faculty and staff. With regard to personal and professional support, this means the leader listens to expressed needs and tries to accommodate and/or facilitate these needs. For example, a leader may work with a teacher to cover her class the last half hour of the day on Mondays so she can take a class, may send a team of inspired teachers to a professional training, or may share information with a teacher interested in school leadership. These are all effective ways to support and grow future leaders.

Domain 3—*Instructional Practices*

Domain 3 defines student achievement as elements of success. Teachers are held accountable for the continued growth of students entrusted to them. Leaders are held accountable for student success on a different level. Teachers are assigned to specific groups of students, such as a self-contained classroom, intervention groups, or recipients of special education services. However, leaders are responsible for all stakeholders within the building or district. This includes students, and faculty, staff, and volunteers who work with the students. The leader has accountability for all programs and services that reach students, all methods used to deliver instruction, and all measurements and monitoring of student progress.

Component 3a—Champions and Supports Curriculum Development

Rationale and Explanation

Common Core State Standards (National Governors Association Center for Best Practices, 2010), hereafter referenced as CCSS, have been a topic of discussion since their development. Initial trainings were held to unpack the standards, gain better understanding of the desired skills, begin CCSS-aligned curriculum development, and identify common resources that would successfully bring us to our end goal—a high level of student achievement. Whether using CCSS or a different set of standards, curriculum must be anchored in and aligned with standards.

Effective leaders demonstrate proactive decision-making, knowing that implementation of initiatives takes time and a commitment of resources. Once the structure is in place, monitoring and adjusting must follow. This calls for continual monitoring of student progress. This can be done in many ways, such as classroom teachers using common assessments. Examples of such assessments are Fountas and Pinnell, Student Intervention Teams (SIT) tracking the progress of students at risk, or longitudinal data such as state tests.

District resources must be equitable and accessible. Common curriculum, common resources, common assessments, and effective teachers should be the core, regardless of the school. Whether a district houses resources in a central location or allocates funds and resources to individual schools, the resources must be known and accessible.

Demonstration

Effective leaders provide the training, scaffolding, and support for staff to implement an initiative successfully. This is an ongoing process that puts the monitoring of student progress at the heart of decision-making. It's not about working harder but working smarter. It's not about how many programs exist in the building but seeing that the ones in place are effective. It's not about buying Common Core State Standards–aligned textbooks or prepackaged programs but meeting the needs of the students through effective use of the resources available. This may mean training paraprofessionals to support interventions, restructuring the schedule to allow blocks for multiage RtI groups, or attending team meetings to engage in professional discussion and planning within grade levels.

Table 2.5. Component 3a: Champions and supports curriculum development

Element	Level of Performance			
	Unsatisfactory	Basic	Proficient	Distinguished
Develops, implements, and revises curriculum	The leader does not develop, implement, or revise curriculum.	The leader inconsistently develops, implements, and revises curriculum.	The leader develops, implements, and revises curriculum reflective of current research.	The leader always develops, implements, and revises curriculum reflective of current research.
Monitors indicators of student success	The leader does not monitor indicators of student success.	The leader inconsistently monitors indicators of student success.	The leader monitors indicators of student success.	The leader always monitors indicators of student success and effectively communicates student progress based on these indicators. She provides direction when student progress is not adequate.
Demands equity and accessibility to curriculum and resources	The leader does not provide equity or accessibility to curriculum and resources.	The leader inconsistently demands equity and accessibility to curriculum and resources.	The leader demands equity and accessibility to curriculum and resources.	The leader always demands equity and accessibility to curriculum and resources that support student achievement.
Refines use of multiple resources for effectiveness	The leader fails to refine use of multiple resources.	The leader inconsistently refines use of multiple resources for effectiveness.	The leader refines use of multiple resources for effectiveness.	The leader always models effective use of multiple resources.
Focuses on quality over quantity	The leader focuses on quantity of curriculum over quality of instruction.	The leader inconsistently demonstrates an understanding of quality of instruction over quantity of curriculum.	The leader demonstrates an understanding of quality instruction over quantity of curriculum.	The leader models and provides accurate and effective direction for depth of understanding over breadth of knowledge.

©Strike (2016).

Table 2.6. Component 3b: Advocates for instruction that supports the needs of all learners

Element	Unsatisfactory	Basic	Proficient	Distinguished
			Level of Performance	
Provides teachers with data to drive instruction and appropriate training to execute	The leader fails to provide data, the use of data to drive instruction or necessary training to execute.	The leader has limited understanding of using data to drive instruction or necessary training to execute.	The leader provides some training for teachers, uses continuous data to analyze and use to drive instruction; provides time for teams to collaborate.	The leader is a model of training on data-driven instruction to all staff; provides time for teams to collaborate; provides continuous data to analyze and execute.
Calls for evidence of alignment between curriculum, instruction, assessment, and professional learning	The leader fails to call for evidence of alignment between curriculum, instruction, assessment, professional learning.	The leader inconsistently calls for evidence of alignment between curriculum, instruction, assessment, and professional learning.	The leader calls for evidence of alignment between curriculum, instruction, assessment, and professional learning; develops and adheres to goals; and articulates the plan.	The leader is a model of alignment between curriculum, instruction, assessment, and professional learning; develops and adheres to goals; and articulates the plan.
Promotes differentiated instruction	The leader fails to promote differentiated instruction.	The leader inconsistently promotes differentiated instruction.	The leader promotes differentiated instruction and provides common planning of instruction to meet the needs of the learner.	The leader is a model of differentiated instruction and provides common planning of instruction to meet the needs of the learner.
Recognizes students as active learners	The leader fails to recognize students as active learners.	The leader inconsistently recognizes students as active learners.	The leader recognizes students as active learners.	The leader always recognizes students as active learners and promotes learning in various ways, which include student input and interests.
Supports instruction that is engaging, rigorous, and relevant	The leader does not support engaging, rigorous, and relevant instruction.	The leader inconsistently supports instruction that is engaging, rigorous, and relevant.	The leader supports instruction that is engaging, rigorous, and relevant; tied to standards; and reflects multiple modalities of learning.	The leader is a model of support for instruction that is engaging, rigorous, and relevant; tied to standards; reflects multiple modalities of learning; and allocates resources to provide high-quality instruction.
Encourages student choice and ownership of one's pathway	The leader does not encourage student choice and ownership of one's pathway.	The leader inconsistently encourages student choice and ownership of one's pathway.	The leader encourages student choice and ownership of one's pathway and coaches teachers to provide multiple opportunities.	The leader is a model of student choice and ownership of one's pathway and coaches teachers to provide multiple opportunities.

Component 3b—Advocates for Instruction That Supports the Needs of All Learners

Rationale and Explanation

Instruction is the catalyst for student achievement, but the puzzle has many pieces. Instruction is the physical, observable piece seen by administrators. Entering a classroom, leadership can tell the objective of the lesson in progress or look at student work and determine the lesson focus.

Just as important to the execution of a good lesson is the planning. Targeted planning reflects several parts, each child specific. Whole-group instruction takes into consideration the exposure to, practice with, and mastery of grade-level skills. Assignments, activities, and projects done as whole group are often differentiated to meet the needs of each child.

It is within a small group that targeted instruction is most effective. Here, the teacher designs lessons specific to students' needs. Teachers must be provided the training, opportunity to participate in discussion with colleagues, and time to both analyze the students' needs and locate resources for the targeted lesson. In addition to classroom instruction and the targeting of student needs, the teacher must work with interventionists and special education teachers to provide more intense services (i.e., Tiers II and III special education services). Documentation and meetings may be required, depending on the RtI process in place by the school/district.

Demonstration

As an instructional watchdog, the leader must ensure that all parents and school personnel understand time allocations; time on task; and the effect of disruptions to classrooms, such as phone calls, PA announcements, or unannounced parent visits.

Analyzing multiple data, teachers must be provided time to plan for targeted instruction. Data retreats provide such opportunity, as do dedicated time with team members, support staff, grade bands, interventionists, and special education personnel.

Component 3c—Analyzes Assessments

Rationale and Explanation

We are in a society where test scores declare a value to the school, district, child's understanding, teacher's performance, and administrator's effectiveness. It is imperative that we use multiple data points that reflect a balanced assessment system (summative, formative, benchmark, interim, and diagnostic assessments). We must look at assessment with regard to what it's testing

Table 2.7. Component 3c: Analyzes assessments

Element	Level of Performance			
	Unsatisfactory	Basic	Proficient	Distinguished
Reflects on and compliments instructional practices	The leader fails to reflect on and compliment instructional practices.	The leader inconsistently reflects on and compliments instructional practices.	The leader reflects on and compliments effective instructional practices and encourages professional conversations that require reflection on current instructional practices.	The leader consistently reflects on and compliments effective instructional practices, coaches teachers to improve instruction continually, provides suggestions to supplement current practices, and encourages professional conversations that require reflection on current instructional practices.
Uses assessment data in ways appropriate to their intended use	The leader fails to demonstrate understanding of assessment data or use it in ways appropriate and intended.	The leader inconsistently demonstrates understanding of assessment data and sometimes uses it in ways appropriate and intended.	The leader demonstrates an understanding of assessment data and usually uses it in ways appropriate and intended.	The leader consistently demonstrates solid understanding of assessment data and always uses it in ways appropriate and intended.
Explores gaps in expectations and opportunities to improve	The leader does not explore gaps in expectations or provide opportunities to improve.	The leader inconsistently explores gaps in expectations and opportunities to improve.	The leader explores gaps in expectations and opportunities to improve.	The leader always explores gaps in expectations and opportunities to improve.
Uses multiple measures of student learning and relevant quality indicators	The leader fails to use multiple measures of student learning and relevant quality indicators.	The leader inconsistently uses multiple measures of student learning and/or has limited understanding of relevant quality indicators.	The leader uses multiple measures of student learning, understands relevant quality indicators, and articulates measures and quality indicators to stakeholders.	The leader always uses multiple measures of student learning, understands relevant quality indicators, and articulates measures and quality indicators to stakeholders. She continually monitors progress of learners relative to measures and indicators.

and how it reflects our students' understanding. We need to ask questions: Does it align with our curriculum (what is taught), does it provide the rigor of instruction (strategies and activities as reflected in the lesson plans), does it provide a relevant format of content evaluation (essay versus multiple choice), and does the test reflect the skills necessary for the students to perform successfully (writing and technological competencies)?

Too often, the public focuses on a test score as a final result when it should be viewed as an ongoing process. It is imperative that leaders understand the type, purpose, and intended uses of each assessment; the data it provides; and how results are reported and to whom. If results come back below grade level or a student demonstrates lack of competency, the leader must explore areas such as gaps in expectations, deficits in student performance, gaps in curriculum, and inconsistencies in delivery of instruction and provide a plan of action for improvement.

Demonstration
For this area to be implemented successfully, teachers need dedicated time set aside on in-service, professional learning, teacher work days, institute days, late start or early dismissal, or other options that work for that particular school. The important factor is that teachers analyze and discuss results; report students' progress to parents and other key stakeholders; and work collaboratively with other teachers, interventionists, and special education personnel to develop a plan to move students to the next level.

Component 3d—Incorporates Technology to Enhance Learning

Rationale and Explanation
Three threads are nonnegotiable when integrating technology: training and professional development of school personnel as needed based on their roles, parent involvement, and dedicated funds in the annual budget (Strike, 2000). These threads are important for the sustainability of successful integration of technology as an initiative so devices and hardware are current and working; teachers and other school personnel assigned to work with the technology are trained in a way that allows them to successfully meet expectations of the district; and parents are both informed and committed to technology's use in the school.

Depending on the structure of the school or district, the integrated technology (IT) support people may be onsite, across several buildings, or district-wide. IT tickets requesting assistance may need to be submitted, or a simple phone call may suffice. To use technology effectively, it must work. If it's down, the downtime must be minimal; therefore, it's imperative to have

Table 2.8. Component 3d: Incorporates technology to enhance learning

Level of Performance

Element	Unsatisfactory	Basic	Proficient	Distinguished
Provides the professional learning/training needed by staff	The leader fails to provide the professional learning/training needed by staff.	The leader inconsistently provides professional learning/training needed by staff.	The leader allocates resources, such as time, talent, and finances, to ensure that he provides the professional learning/training needed by staff.	The leader consistently seeks out opportunities for professional development and training for staff and demonstrates an understanding of impact on student learners.
Dedicates fiscal resources for the upgrade, purchase, and ongoing training needed by staff	The leader fails to dedicate fiscal resources for the upgrade, purchase, and ongoing training needed by staff.	The leader inconsistently dedicates fiscal resources for the upgrade, purchase, and ongoing training needed by staff.	The leader dedicates resources for the upgrade, purchase, and ongoing training. Commitment is evident through allocation of fiscal resources and providing ongoing training needed by staff.	The leader consistently dedicates resources for the upgrade, purchase, and ongoing training. Commitment is evident through allocation of fiscal resources and providing ongoing training needed by staff.
Expects integration of technology for a 21st-century education	The leader fails to expect integration of technology for a 21st-century education.	The leader inconsistently expects integration of technology for a 21st-century education.	The leader expects integration of technology for a 21st-century education; coaches teachers and/or provides training in areas of technology for teachers to integrate within lessons for both delivery of instruction and interactive lessons.	The leader is a model of integration of technology for a 21st-century education; coaches teachers and/or provides training in areas of technology for teachers to integrate within lessons for both delivery of instruction and interactive lessons.
Oversees programs and license compliance	The leader fails to oversee programs and/or license compliance.	The leader inconsistently oversees programs and license compliance.	The leader oversees programs and license compliance.	The leader always oversees programs and license compliance effectively and works collaboratively with technology support staff.
Commits to timely technology support	The leader fails to commit to timely technology support.	The leader inconsistently commits to timely technology support.	The leader commits to and intervenes effectively to ensure timely technology support.	The leader always commits to and intervenes effectively to ensure timely technology support through talent and finances.

sufficient IT personnel to cover the needs of the district, and those persons must be knowledgeable and responsive.

Finally, there are many choices of programs and applications. The district/ school must be very careful here. It's easy to overextend finances, time, and bandwidth for applications or programs that look good or are fun. Remember, every program or application chosen must be aligned with the set curriculum, meet criteria set by the school/district, be affordable, and have both short-term and long-range sustainability. As a school/district, be sure your IT persons and administrators are well aware of licensing fees, including length of the license and how many students, seats, or computers the license covers.

Demonstration

Leadership must collaborate and communicate openly to ensure that teachers and other personnel working with technology are appropriately trained to meet the expectations of the school. This includes ongoing training for updates and new initiatives. Technologies become obsolete quickly, districts often differ from building to building in what is offered, and teachers will enter the school at different levels of competency and comfort. Be sure to offer trainings for teachers and other personnel arriving midyear, such as student management systems, SMART boards, calendars and appointments, and classroom websites.

Summary

This chapter focuses on Domains 2 and 3 of *The Leadership Framework*. Under Domain 2, we explore the knowledge, skills, dispositions, and practices required in leaders specific to professional learning and growth practices. Under Domain 3 we explore the knowledge, skills, dispositions, and practices specific to instructional practices.

Each rubric provides specific indicators. Following the rubrics are narrative descriptors to further enhance understanding of the expectations of each indicator. Evaluation is an active process through which the person evaluated knows the expectations, has descriptive narration of the expectations, and is provided specific feedback. The person evaluated has the opportunity to see the rubric prior to the evaluation process and place himself or herself within the context of the rubric with justification and evidence of that placement. The evaluator also has the opportunity to place the person evaluated in the rubric with justification and evidence. The two have a professional conversation based on placement on the rubrics. Professional goals are established based on the placement, with a plan to monitor, provide evidence of progress, and reevaluate.

Case Studies

Case Study #1

Terrance is a teacher and an aspiring principal. He expressed an interest in moving into a leadership role while in your building. As an effective leader yourself, you have assisted Terrance through shared leadership by helping him find a quality educational leadership program, setting him up for success during his practicum, placing him in teacher leadership roles, providing opportunities for him to assume leadership roles, developing PLCs, working on a teacher advisory council, and having him serve as the administrator in charge in your absence.

All indicators show that Terrance is phenomenal in the classroom, but the transition to working in the leadership capacity has not been smooth. Upon your return after Terrance served as your substitute, faculty and parents flood you with complaints of inconsistency in handling classroom issues with students. Without his support, staff shared the feeling that it's a waste of time sending students to the office when nothing is done. Although he makes decisions, staff is unsure of the basis for his decisions. When confronted, Terrance becomes defensive that he's being challenged in his new role.

Discussion Questions for Case Study #1

1. Who identifies the components and elements for the professional discussion?
2. If you observed the scenario above, how would your professional discussion begin?
3. What would you highlight as strengths?
4. What would you bring to light as areas of necessary improvement?
5. What type of evidence would you look for in future observations to determine growth in the identified areas of necessary improvement?

Case Study #2

Tia is a veteran administrator who has served in the field for 25 years, 15 of which have been in leadership roles. Tia is at the building at 7:15 when the doors open for breakfast for her students. While students are eating, she talks with them, finding out what has taken place in their lives over the weekend or overnight. She then meets up with teachers who have arrived, often serving as a listening ear or holding meetings before the school day begins. When the entrance bell rings, Tia stands in the front foyer greeting each student—often by name.

Announcements take place immediately, and the intercom goes silent until the end of the day. If Tia needs to communicate with a teacher, she sends him an e-mail so he can respond at his convenience. If urgent, she will walk down to the classroom or call the teacher.

At some point during the day, depending on her schedule, Tia announces to the office staff she's going for a walk and she quietly enters each classroom, fulfilling her motto: *every classroom—every day*. She often quietly asks one or two students what they are learning about in that lesson. She sometimes serves as an extra set of hands or eyes, answering questions or helping a student solve a problem while the teacher is working with another student.

Students often ask Tia if they can have lunch with her; if her schedule is clear, she invites the student to join her in her office. Tia talks to the classroom teacher, and if the student is behind, she asks the student to bring work to provide one-on-one tutoring; however, if the student is caught up on work, she invites her to bring a friend. Tia enjoys this time with students as she gets to know them on a personal level.

When Tia joined the staff, the school had many deficits. It lacked curriculum, common resources, and alignment to any set of standards. Lesson planning was not required, assessments were not triangulated, no interventions or monitoring system were in place, and teachers had never been evaluated. Over the course of two years, Tia worked with groups of teachers to address these deficits within the school; however, not all teachers are happy with the changes.

In an effort to continue professional dialogue and create more buy-in, Tia attends grade-level PLC meetings by invitation or places herself on their agenda when she sees a need. She has ongoing discussions with the grade-level lead teacher regarding fidelity of initiatives and following curriculum. From these meetings, she identifies professional development opportunities.

Discussion Questions for Case Study #2

1. Who identifies the components and elements for the professional discussion?
2. If the above scenario were your observation, how would your professional discussion begin?
3. What would you highlight as strengths?
4. What would you bring to light as areas of necessary improvement?
5. What type of evidence would you look for in future observations to determine growth in the identified areas of necessary improvement?

Self-Assessment and Reflection

Reread the two case studies, making note of specific knowledge, skills, dispositions, and practices observed in each leader. Choose three and align those identified skills with indicators on the rubric. Note that the first case study reflects a novice administrator, the second, a veteran. Consider how this experience affects not only the placement on the rubric but also the professional conversation.

Then, do the same for yourself. If you told your story or captured your leadership journey to date, what skills would be evident? Choose three and align those identified skills with indicators on the rubric. If an area of strength, is it consistent or situational? If an area of deficit, what might you do to address it? What resources might you need? What evidence would you use to determine growth in this area?

References

Bolman, L., & Deal, T. (2001). *Leading with soul: An uncommon journey of spirit.* San Francisco, CA: Jossey-Bass.

Danielson, C. (2007). *Enhancing professional practice: A framework for teaching.* Alexandria, VA: Association of Supervision and Curriculum Development.

Foley, E., Mishook, J., Thompson, J., Kubiak, M., Supovitz, J., & Rhude-Faust, M. (2008). *Beyond test scores: Leading indicators for education.* Providence, RI: Brown University's Annenberg Institute for School Reform.

Garmston, R., & Wellman, B. (2013). *The adaptive school: A sourcebook for developing collaborative groups.* Lanham, MD: Rowman & Littlefield.

Gruenert, S., & Whitaker, T. (2015). *School culture rewired: How to define, assess and transform it.* Alexandria, VA: Association of Supervision and Curriculum Development.

Killion, J. (2011, June). A bold move forward. *The Learning Professional, 32*(3), 10–14.

Knight, J. (2018). *The impact cycle.* Thousand Oaks, CA: Corwin.

National Governors Association Center for Best Practices & Council of Chief State School Officers. (2010). *Common Core State Standards.* Washington DC: National Governors Association Center for Best Practices & Council of Chief State School Officers.

Strike, K. (2000). *Technology's role in blue ribbon schools.* Milwaukee, WI: Marquette University.

Yukl, G., & Gardner, W. III. (2020). *Leadership in organizations.* (9th ed.). Boston, MA: Pearson Education, Inc.

~

CHAPTER THREE

The Framework for Effective Leadership

Domains 1 and 4

We believe that leadership is important and that the most effective leadership is informed, deeply developed, and widely distributed.

—Garmston & Wellman (2013)

Objectives

At the conclusion of this chapter you will be able to:

1. Distinguish the role of the leader in developing, articulating, implementing, and stewarding a vision of learning that is shared and supported by all stakeholders (PSEL 1, 10; NELP 1).
2. Promote a positive school culture that advocates, nurtures, and sustains student success and the professional growth and development of staff (PSEL 4, 5, 6, 7; NELP 2, 3, 4, 7).
3. Critique management of the organization, operation, and resources for a safe, efficient, and effective learning environment (PSEL 9; NELP 6).
4. Promote collaboration with stakeholders and respond to needs of a diverse community through mobilization of community resources (PSEL 8, 9; NELP 5, 6).
5. Promote the success of every student by acting with integrity and fairness and in an ethical manner (PSEL 2, 3; NELP 2, 5).

6. Respond to and influence the political, social, economic, legal, and cultural context that affects student learning, and anticipate and assess emerging trends and initiatives in order to adapt leadership strategies (PSEL 3, 8; NELP 2, 3, 5).

Expectations and Introspection—Domains 1 and 4

This chapter examines the collective characteristics of effective leaders through the form of rubrics and narrative descriptors. The indicators within each rubric reflect leadership standards of PSEL (2015), NELP (2018), and Learning Forward. A crosswalk of the standards and the leadership framework appears in chapter 5.

"A particularly noteworthy finding is the empirical link between school leadership and improved student achievement" (Wallace Foundation, 2011, p. 3). "Leadership is second only to classroom instruction among all school-related factors that contribute to what students learn at school" (NASSP, 2013, p. 5). The question of what good leadership looks like or how we define good leadership differs in literature based on the perspective and lens through which it's viewed. Through the identification and explanation of the knowledge, skills, dispositions, and practices of educational leaders, we've unpacked an intertwined system to create a common foundation of understanding. Through this lens we better understand the characteristics, their relationship to each other, and their effect on schools, personnel, and students.

In Sergiovanni's (1992) work, *Moral Leadership: Getting to the Heart of School Improvement*, he states, "Instead of relying on rules, personality or interpersonal skills, leaders will be able to rely on standards of practice and professional norms as reasons for doing things. Leadership itself will become less direct and intense as standards and norms take hold" (p. 40). Though Sergiovanni's insightful work dates back more than 20 years, the premise of establishing norms and standards of practice for educational leaders was not solidified until now.

A foundational principle of leadership is that "Leaders are responsible for building the capacity in individuals, teams and organizations to be leaders and learners" (Killian, 2011, p. 11). Fullan (2011) reminds us "the conventional wisdom about power of the leader has included human capital or cumulative abilities, knowledge and skills developed through formal education and on-the-job experience" (p. 4).

But we must expand our approach to effective leadership and recognize social capital that resides in relationships. In his keynote presentation *Social Capital*, Andrew Hargreaves explains it as "how we labor together, plan, teach, look at student work, collaborate—TRUST—high trust leads to high performance . . . it's a causal relationship . . . Social capital raises human capital—you will improve if surrounded by good colleagues" (presentation at the Wisconsin State Reading Association Annual Convention, Milwaukee, February 2015). In 1971, R. J. House theorized that "the behavior of leaders has an effect on the performance and satisfaction levels of followers" (as cited in Green, 2016, p. 41).

These words remind us that humans are social beings. We are not meant to live life alone but to interact socially: to teach, learn, and grow from one another. We are not meant to be in isolation but in community. To experience growth in this manner, we must discard the idea that it's dangerous to express vulnerability to our colleagues or supervisors for fear it will take away professional status, imply judgment, or make us look bad. Continual improvement calls for reflection, open and honest communication, and the opportunity to participate in ongoing dialogue with peers to enrich and amplify professional learning and growth.

Hargreaves and Fullan (2008) state, "The last frontier of instructional improvement is getting behind the classroom door," and they note, "Deprivatizing teaching involves opening the world of the classroom to scrutiny and continuous development of instruction" (p. 23). They cite Barber and Mourshed of McKinsey and Company, who drew this conclusion: "The top performing school systems recognized that the only way to improve outcomes is to improve instruction . . . they understood which interventions were effective to improve instruction—coaching, practical teacher training, developing stronger school leaders, and enabling teachers to learn from each other—and then found ways to deliver those interventions across their school systems" (as cited in Hargreaves & Fullan, 2008, p. 26).

Effective leadership calls for shared, horizontal, or distributed leadership. Jones, Harvey, Lefoe, and Ryland (2013) describe distributive leadership in this way:

> Distributed Leadership for learning and teaching is a leadership approach in which collaborative working is undertaken between individuals who trust and respect each other's contribution. It occurs as a result of an open culture within and across an institution. It is an approach in which reflective practice is an integral part enabling actions to be critiqued, challenged and developed through cycles of planning, action, reflection and assessment and

replanning. It happens most effectively when people at all levels engage in action, accepting leadership in their particular areas of expertise. It requires resources that support and enable collaborative environments together with a flexible approach to space, time and finance which occur as a result of diverse contextual settings in an institution. Through shared and active engagement, distributed leadership can result in the development of leadership capacity to sustain improvements in teaching and learning. (p. 21)

As leaders, we have both direct and indirect influence. We need both "precision of practice and transparency of both practice and its connection to results . . . to build into ongoing cultures" (Hargreaves & Fullan, 2008, p. 27). "In short, leading knowledgeably is at the core of all highly effective organizations. It is worth fighting for because it is extremely hard to achieve and yet is essential. Knowledge is literally the substance of change. It represents the means of all accomplishments" (p. 31).

According to Hersey and Blanchard (1982), "To be effective, the leader must take into consideration the followers' maturity level . . . [which is] the extent to which a follower demonstrates the ability to perform a task [job maturity] and his or her willingness to accept responsibility [motivational level] for its completion" (as cited in Green, 2016, p. 42). These two dimensions, task and relationship, along with the condition of the relationships among the leader, the follower, and the situation, allow the leader to elect from one of four styles: directing, coaching, supporting, or delegating. We know this as situational leadership.

Leadership is more caught than taught. Leaders must be knowledgeable yet balance influence. Motives eventually determine direction, so leaders must keep in check. They relinquish the thought of personal gain and embrace their success through the people they've taught. A leader who seeks personal gain stirs division, while a leader who builds capacity equips and shares possibilities with other gifted people who will carry on beyond his tenure. Effective leaders give away credit for victories rather than hoarding for self-glorification or recognition. Leaders must energize others and create collaborative cultures yet remain accountable. Although this list is not comprehensive, it demonstrates the complexity of effective leadership.

Rubrics

The overall discussion on rubrics, general descriptors, and levels of performance provided in chapter 2 applies equally to Domains 1 and 4 in chapter 3. Domain 1 focuses on *Leadership Competencies*, and Domain 4 focuses on

Management Competencies. When speaking about leadership or management, there are different styles, and each presents positive and negative attributes.

The Leadership Framework does not focus on one style of leadership or on characteristics, traits, or behaviors of leaders (or managers) working within that style. Instead, it identifies knowledge, skills, dispositions, and practices of effective leaders. One framework is sufficient for all leaders. Experienced leaders need to exemplify the same skills as novices but should do so at an advanced level and with automaticity; therefore, experienced leaders are not called to complete greater tasks than novices but to demonstrate greater skill to successfully complete the tasks.

Domain 1—*Leadership Competencies*

Domain 1 reflects the foundational knowledge, skills, dispositions, and practices in which an effective leader must demonstrate competence. These are the critical components and foundational building blocks of effective leaders. Just as a building must be built on a secure foundation, so must effective leadership. Should these areas be shaky or cracked, expect chaos, dysfunction, and a negative effect on performance. It is only when leaders demonstrate mastery of these foundational skills that they expound the flexibility, responsiveness, and maximization of resources that provide an environment in which all stakeholders function as a single entity toward a shared vision.

Component 1a—Establishes a Solid Foundation

Rationale and Explanation
The foundational principles of the school must be public, known, and upheld. If the mission, vision, values, and goals of the school or district are merely a piece of paper, a quote in the handbook, or a banner on the wall, then they are a passive part of school culture. Everyone—parents, teachers, faculty, staff, and administration—should not only know these principles but exemplify them. School personnel must extend beyond knowledge of these statements and validate their importance through visible actions throughout daily life within the school. This is absolutely foundational to the inner workings and expectations of the school/district.

Another foundational piece to the inner workings of the school is the approach leadership takes to change. In an article titled "Change Leader, Change Thyself," Boaz and Fox (2014) state:

Table 3.1. Component 1a: Establishes a solid foundation

| | Level of Performance | | | |
Element	Unsatisfactory	Basic	Proficient	Distinguished
Develops and upholds the mission, vision, values, and goals of the school	The leader does not work to develop or uphold the mission, vision, values, and goals of the school.	The leader inconsistently develops and upholds the mission, vision, values, and goals of the school.	The leader develops and upholds the mission, vision, values, and goals of the school.	The leader effectively develops and upholds the mission, vision, values, and goals of the school.
Identifies benchmarks, expectations, and feedback measures to ensure accountability	The leader fails to identify benchmarks, expectations, and feedback measures to ensure accountability.	The leader inconsistently identifies benchmarks, expectations, and feedback measures to ensure accountability.	The leader identifies benchmarks, expectations, and feedback measures to ensure accountability.	The leader effectively identifies benchmarks, expectations, and feedback measures to ensure accountability.
Acts as a decision maker	The leader fails to or avoids making decisions.	The leader sporadically makes decisions.	The leader regularly makes decisions.	The leader models consistent decision making.
Serves as a change agent	The leader does not act as a change agent.	The leader occasionally acts as a change agent.	The leader demonstrates the ability to be a change agent.	The leader consistently models the role of change agent.
Builds caring and effective relationships with stakeholders	The leader does not build caring and effective relationships with stakeholders.	The leader inconsistently builds caring and effective relationships with stakeholders.	The leader usually demonstrates caring and effective relationship with stakeholders.	The leader is a model of and demonstrates a caring and effective relationship with stakeholders.
Practices accessible, approachable, and engaged role in school	The leader is not accessible, approachable, and engaged in the school.	The leader is rarely accessible, approachable, or engaged in the school.	The leader is usually accessible, approachable, and engaged in the school.	The leader is always accessible, approachable, and engaged in the school.
Epitomizes resilience	The leader is not resilient and/or may overreact.	The leader is inconsistently resilient and may lack composure.	The leader demonstrates resiliency and composure.	The leader is a model of composure and resiliency.

To achieve collective change over time, actions . . . are necessary but seldom sufficient. A new strategy will fall short of its potential if it fails to address the underlying mind-sets and capabilities of the people who will execute it . . . half of all efforts to transform organizational performance fail either because senior managers don't act as role models for change or because people in the organization defend the status quo. In other words, despite the stated change goals, people on the ground tend to behave as they did before. (p. 4)

In an era when change is frequent and mandatory and has a great impact on staff, procedures, policies, and budget, the call is to balance support and accountability. Some leaders face change in a proactive manner, some in a reactive way, and some function at status quo. Leaders acknowledge, encourage, redirect, teach, model, and build capacity in others. Leaders plan, guide, instruct, equip, provide and allocate resources, and support. Some leaders are charismatic or focus on the relational aspects of leadership. Some project a shared or distributed leadership style and are inclusive in nature. Others demonstrate transformational leadership or may be more direct in nature. The pathways are many to the destination of a successful school.

The adoption of Common Core State Standards (CCSS) transformed instruction in some schools while others made no movement at all to align standards, curriculum, assessment, and professional learning. Though the CCSS have been opposed by several states, standards of some type (i.e., Smarter Balance, Partnership for Assessment of Readiness for College and Careers, State Standards) have been adopted. With this, awareness of and debates about high stakes testing, validity, reliability, and alignment to the standards have heightened. Connected to this is accountability of districts, schools, administration, and teachers, with performance evaluations and value-added growth measures reliant on student test scores.

With changes in education, leaders may find themselves—or discern they have a gift and calling—to serve as a turnaround leader. Effective leadership in a turnaround school is one of four tenets, with the others being instructional transformation, talent development, and culture shift. Jackson, Fixsen, and Ward (2018) describe:

The policies, structures, resources, and personnel that leaders put in place to rapidly and significantly improve the schools reflect the leaders' strong commitment to this work. Turnaround leaders catalyze and organize the coordinated work of the staff charged with implementing efforts to rapidly improve schools, harnessing their efforts and drawing them to a shared vision of success. (p. 4)

Leo Tolstoy wrote, "Everyone thinks of changing the world, but no one thinks of changing himself" (Boaz & Fox, 2014, p. 1). An effective leader must look inward and outward at the process of change. Leaders must look at their own beliefs, priorities, aspirations, values, fears, biases, and prejudices while addressing technical aspects, such as training, adaptations, and rollout of implementation. "Our leadership will always be most natural, most effective, and most influential when we lead from our gifts and strengths" (Maxwell & Elmore, 2007, p. 1508).

Demonstration
An effective leader must be able to communicate, disseminate, delegate, supervise, and ensure that policies, procedures, and initiatives are met with fidelity while operating within the budget and resources provided. Knowledge and understanding, approachability, accessibility, and resiliency are necessary skills of an effective leader.

Component 1b—Builds Shared Leadership

Rationale and Explanation
Effective leaders put their own advancement aside and advocate for staff and students. They are collaborative and build shared leadership. When educational leaders lead with authority, the top-down approach leaves little to no room for shared leadership. Shared leadership has many benefits, including buy-in from stakeholders; open communication; shared problem-solving; support of current staff; creation or molding of future leaders; recognition of individuals' strengths as an asset to a collective benefit; and retention of staff.

Shared leadership promotes discussion and collaboration. Rather than reporting what will be done and how, decisions are made through dialogue and consensus. Leadership appointments may change based on the problem or project at hand and take into consideration the person's knowledge, experience, and interests. Novice leaders receive support needed as they experience a learning curve with new or expanded duties assigned to them. No one needs to feel isolated; in shared leadership you function as a collective group.

The shared leadership theory can work in collaboration and not competition with distributed leadership. "Viewing leadership in terms of reciprocal, recursive influence processes among multiple leaders is different from studying unidirectional effects of a single leader on subordinates" (Yukl & Gardner, 2020, p. 188).

Table 3.2.   Component 1b: Builds shared leadership

Element	Level of Performance			
	Unsatisfactory	Basic	Proficient	Distinguished
Advocates for staff and students	The leader does not advocate for staff and students.	The leader advocates ineffectively for staff and students with little success or advocates for one group but not both.	The leader advocates for staff and students with some success.	The leader is a model of and advocates effectively for staff and students.
Works collaboratively with stakeholders	The leader works in isolation without the input of appropriate stakeholders.	The leader rarely works in collaboration with appropriate stakeholders.	The leader works collaboratively with appropriate stakeholders.	The leader is a model of working with appropriate stakeholders in a collaborative manner.
Promotes development of teacher and administrative leaders	The leader does not support the development of teacher and administrative leaders.	The leader inconsistently promotes the development of teacher and administrative leaders.	The leader frequently promotes development of teacher and administrative leaders.	The leader actively seeks out opportunities for development for teacher and administrative leaders.
Delegates tasks based on interests and skill sets	The leader delegates tasks without consideration of skill sets and interests of the designee.	The leader gives little consideration to interests and skill sets of designees.	The leader usually gives consideration to the interests and skill sets of designees.	The leader always gives consideration and evaluation of skill sets and interests prior to delegating tasks.
Builds consensus with appropriate stakeholders	The leader acts independently without consensus of appropriate stakeholders.	The leader builds consensus with appropriate stakeholders in an inconsistent manner.	The leader builds consensus with appropriate stakeholders.	The leader models and seeks many opportunities to build consensus with appropriate stakeholders.
Supports innovative thinking and risk-taking efforts	The leader does not support innovative thinking and risk-taking efforts.	The leader sometimes supports innovative thinking and risk-taking efforts.	The leader supports innovative thinking and risk-taking efforts.	The leader actively supports and rewards innovative thinking and risk-taking efforts.

Distributed leadership is not delegation of work, but "collective work as well as collective learning by working on goals through communication and interaction is prominent, rather than individual work" (Halverson, 2007, as cited in Goksoy, 2016). An example of distributed leadership is building capacity of one teacher by another (Copeland, 2003, as cited in Goksoy, 2016). Support through mentoring and coaching in particular are ways to identify and develop skills in prospective, new, or novice teachers.

Demonstration

Trust and respect are foundational to working as a unit rather than individually. This calls for leaders in key positions to be knowledgeable and comfortable enough with their own performance, strengths, and deficits to step back and share duties and responsibilities. We must reject micromanagement and make open communication common practice. Gradual release of responsibility is an effective way to move from an authoritative model to distributed or shared leadership. Examples can be asking a teacher to facilitate a staff meeting, run a peer training, or undertake small leadership roles to provide stepping-stones for teacher leadership.

Component 1c—Initiates Effective Communication

Rationale and Explanation

Communication is absolutely essential to effective leadership. Verbal and written communications in the public forum are judged on choice and effectiveness of words. Using poor grammar, slang, curse words, or politically incorrect statements are quick ways to articulate a lack of professionalism and may lead to a loss of respect or nonrenewal.

When trouble brews, often miscommunication or lack of communication is at its center; therefore, communication must be timely, open, and clear. Adhere to calendars, meetings, and events, and begin functions on time. This provides a sense of respect for the stakeholder's time as well as continuity and comfort in making the expectations known.

Providing responses in a timely manner is essential. Based on role, district or school policy, climate and culture, make the response timetable public. Communication includes but is not limited to returning e-mails and phone calls within 24 hours of receiving them; changing messages, voice mail, and e-mail to reflect out-of-office status and responding to communication in a timely manner upon return; providing contact information in case of emergency; and identifying to staff a tiered order of whom to contact in an urgent situation.

Table 3.3. Component 1c: Initiates effective communication

Element	Unsatisfactory	Basic	Proficient	Distinguished
		Level of Performance		
Uses verbal, nonverbal, and written means effectively	The leader uses inappropriate verbal, nonverbal, and written communication.	The leader uses ineffective verbal, nonverbal, and written communication.	The leader uses acceptable verbal, nonverbal, and written communication.	The leader models effective verbal, nonverbal, and written communication.
Articulates programs, progress, and needs	The leader fails to articulate programs, progress, and needs.	The leader sometimes articulates programs, progress, and needs.	The leader usually articulates programs, progress, and needs.	The leader models effective articulation of programs, progress, and needs.
Recognizes and celebrates accomplishments of students and staff	The leader fails to recognize and celebrate the accomplishments of students and staff.	The leader selectively recognizes and celebrates the accomplishments of students and staff.	The leader usually recognizes and celebrates the accomplishments of students and staff.	The leader always recognizes and celebrates the accomplishments of students and staff.
Facilitates professional dialogue	The leader fails to facilitate professional dialogue.	The leader occasionally facilitates professional dialogue.	The leader usually facilitates professional dialogue.	The leader models, facilitates, and embraces professional dialogue.
Promotes identification, analysis, and use of creative solutions to problems	The leader fails to identify, analyze, or use creative solutions.	The leader sometimes promotes identification, analysis, and use of creative solutions.	The leader usually promotes identification, analysis, and use of creative solutions.	The leader models an active role in the identification, analysis, and use of creative solutions.
Considers all opinions in a respectful and open manner	The leader does not consider all opinions in a respectful and open manner.	The leader inconsistently considers all opinions in a respectful and open manner.	The leader usually considers all opinions in a respectful and open manner.	The leader always considers opinions in a respectful and open manner.
Elicits others' opinions in decision making	The leader does not elicit others' opinions in decision making.	The leader occasionally elicits others' opinions in decision making.	The leader usually elicits others' opinions in decision making.	The leader always elicits others' opinions actively in decision making.

©Strike (2016).

As a leader, clearly, appropriately, and accurately report programs, progress, and needs to stakeholders. Sharing this information is imperative as a community, both to celebrate successes and to address deficits whether they involve academics, finances, or personnel. Acknowledge personal and professional accomplishments of staff and students. Schools often recognize students with student of the month, character or PBIS rewards, tokens, and treats. Personnel often go above and beyond the call of duty with no additional compensation or recognition but for the good of the students, so it is important to remember to celebrate faculty and staff accomplishments and distinguished acts too.

Demonstration
Effective leaders clearly communicate through a variety of channels to reach multiple stakeholders (i.e., use of a messenger system through student management to send out voice messages, e-mails, or texts). The marquee shares information in a quick way to the community. Other quick and easy communication can be shared through a school newsletter or district website that is updated regularly. A local newspaper can list upcoming events as well as report on activities and events that have happened. Parent contact logs can track school contacts (e.g., classroom teacher, specialist, or dean of students), phone calls, and e-mails to parents or guardians.

Component 1d—Adheres to a Moral Compass

Rationale and Explanation
By nature, the concept of a moral compass is highly subjective. Involvement in community, district, school, or outside activities presents various challenges that can make or break a leader, regardless of his performance. Using ethical judgment, based on honesty, integrity, respect, fairness, consistency, or follow-through, creates one's reputation. The type of community where one resides and serves directly affects judgment and tolerance of one's morality.

Demonstration
In educational leadership, the metaphor of being in a fishbowl is sometimes used. This references that our actions, thoughts, and words are public. Social media plays a role in determining a person's character based on relationships, comments, or pictures posted. The reality is that educators are public servants and always *on*, whether at a school, district, or private event.

Table 3.4. Component 1d: Adheres to a moral compass

Element	Level of Performance			
	Unsatisfactory	Basic	Proficient	Distinguished
Models integrity, fairness, honesty, and respect	The leader fails to model integrity, fairness, honesty, and respect.	The leader sometimes models integrity, fairness, honesty, and respect.	The leader is fair, honest and respectful and maintains a high level of integrity.	The leader always models integrity, fairness, honesty, and respect.
Maintains professional dispositions	The leader fails to maintain professional dispositions.	The leader occasionally maintains professional dispositions.	The leader demonstrates professional dispositions.	The leader is a model of effective professional dispositions.
Works for educational and not personal gain	The leader works for personal rather than educational gain.	The leader inconsistently works for educational gain.	The leader usually works for educational gain.	The leader is a model of working for educational gain.
Demonstrates the application of ethics and justice	The leader fails to apply ethics and justice to daily work.	The leader inconsistently applies ethics and justice to daily work.	The leader applies ethics and justice in educational and personal life.	The leader models effective application of ethics and justice in educational and personal life.
Models and applies an understanding of the cultural context of the community	The leader fails to model or apply understanding of the cultural context of the community.	The leader inconsistently models an understanding of the cultural context of the community.	The leader regularly models and applies an understanding of the cultural context of the community.	The leader models and applies an effective understanding of the cultural context of the community.
Encourages and inspires others to higher levels of commitment, performance, and motivation	The leader does not encourage or act as an inspiration to others to increase commitment, performance, and/or motivation.	The leader is inconsistent in efforts to inspire others to higher levels of commitment, performance, and motivation.	The leader encourages and inspires others to higher levels of commitment, performance, and motivation.	The leader effectively seeks out opportunities to encourage and inspire others to higher levels of commitment, performance, and motivation.

©Strike (2016).

Component 1e—Promotes a Positive School Culture

Rationale and Explanation

A safe, educationally sound climate allows students to be comfortable and maximize their educational experience. Stakeholders must know and feel a response to their needs. In addition, fairness, equity, and diversity need to be evident. This means, regardless of income, race, ethnicity, special needs or interventions, levels of parent volunteerism, position (e.g., board member), or donation, each child is treated as if he or she is *the* most important child in the school.

An effective leader uses every aspect of the school day to participate actively in the lives of students. Through presence, visibility, and accessibility, leaders can avoid escalation of situations, stop fights, address bullying, observe teaching and learning styles, build relationships with teachers and students, and keep an ongoing pulse of the school. Visibility of a leader includes an active and physical presence on the playground, in hallways, bathrooms, and classrooms; greeting staff and students in the front foyer; walking students to their buses or assisting with parent pickup; making rounds through the lunchroom; escorting a student for a needed time-out; or redirecting a student to help him or her make a better choice. Through the leader's actions, the tone is set with regard to an environment that exhibits trust, tolerance, respect, and rapport with stakeholders.

Demonstration

Upon entering a school building, there is an immediate sensory reaction. One can tell a lot just from interactions near the reception desk, front office, and foyer. For example, was it easy to locate visitor parking and know which door to enter? Is the front foyer welcoming to parents? Is it welcoming to visitors? Is it easy to locate the school office? If asked to wait, is student work on the walls to view? Is there a comfortable place to sit? Was a beverage offered to the guest? Are the adult restrooms clearly marked? Is the area clean? Is it noisy or chaotic? Do visitors overhear conversations from the front office staff or between teachers that should be held in private?

Domain 4—*Management Competencies*

Domain 4 reflects the nuts and bolts, the daily grind, or the behind-the-scenes requirements to run a school or district. This domain focuses on policies, procedures, and practices in place to manage the school or district effectively and efficiently. A critical consideration of effective leadership is

Table 3.5. Component 1e: Promotes a positive school culture

Element	Level of Performance			
	Unsatisfactory	Basic	Proficient	Distinguished
Establishes an environment of trust, tolerance, respect, and rapport	The leader fails to establish an environment of trust, tolerance, respect, and rapport.	The leader inconsistently establishes an environment of trust, tolerance, respect, and rapport.	The leader establishes an environment of trust, tolerance, respect, and rapport.	The leader models and establishes an environment of trust, tolerance, respect, and rapport.
Advocates equity, fairness, and diversity	The leader fails to model equity, fairness, and diversity.	The leader inconsistently advocates equity, fairness, and diversity.	The leader advocates equity, fairness, and diversity.	The leader effectively advocates equity, fairness, and diversity.
Sustains safe and educationally sound climate	The leader does not sustain a safe and educationally sound climate.	The leader sometimes works to sustain a safe and educationally sound climate.	The leader sustains a safe and educationally sound climate.	The leader is a model of and effectively sustains a safe and educationally sound climate.
Responds to needs of stakeholders	The leader fails to respond to the needs of stakeholders.	The leader inconsistently responds to the needs of stakeholders.	The leader responds appropriately to the needs of stakeholders.	The leader always responds appropriately to the needs of stakeholders.
Demonstrates cultural responsiveness	The leader fails to demonstrate cultural responsiveness.	The leader rarely demonstrates cultural responsiveness.	The leader regularly demonstrates cultural responsiveness.	The leader always models and demonstrates cultural responsiveness.
Encourages inquiry and reflection	The leader fails to encourage or support inquiry and reflection.	The leader inconsistently encourages inquiry and reflection.	The leader often encourages inquiry and reflection.	The leader seeks out opportunities to encourage inquiry and reflection.

©Strike (2016).

reporting in a timely and accurate manner. The resourcefulness of the leader is examined within the components of this domain.

Component 4a—Adheres to Personnel Requirements

Rationale and Explanation

The district incurs a cost each time a person is hired. That cost not only includes the new hire's wages and benefits but also advertising costs for postings, the search committee's time to screen and interview, HR's time for paperwork and reference checks, and board members' time to study candidates. New employees have a learning curve and need time to acclimate to the new environment, new rules, new students, new colleagues, and new parents and families. A review of literature in the business field affirms that it takes three years to become productive in a new position.

We also know that students' performance is affected directly when they are placed with ineffective teachers. The first year is recoverable, and the second year is partially recoverable; after the third year of ineffective teaching, the student will have irreconcilable deficits. It is imperative that educational leaders recruit, train, support, and retain highly competent personnel.

Effective educational leaders provide an evaluation process that focuses on the continual growth of school personnel. Each individual has areas of strength that can be identified. To evaluate school personnel effectively, we must look at each component of teaching and provide specific feedback to break down the art of teaching into manageable, identifiable parts. We then work with staff to build knowledge and skills that enhance the areas of deficit, coach for improvement, and celebrate the areas of accomplishment.

Demonstration

Evaluation of staff requires many skills on the part of the leader. One must build a level of trust and respect to enter classrooms, provide feedback, and move staff to be receptive to recommendations. To be viewed as a credible evaluator, one must be knowledgeable about the content observed, instructional strategies, assessment, and communication of information to students. One must be consistent and fair, sharing the expectations (rubric or evaluation form) up front and communicating the process effectively. Finally, one must show respect toward the person evaluated, such as arriving on time for the scheduled evaluation and not judging a person's competency but supporting and coaching the person to success.

Table 3.6. Component 4a: Adheres to personnel requirements

		Level of Performance		
Element	Unsatisfactory	Basic	Proficient	Distinguished
Recruits, trains, supports, and retains highly competent personnel	The leader fails to recruit, train, support, or retain highly competent personnel.	The leader inconsistently recruits, trains, supports, or retains highly competent personnel.	The leader recruits, trains, supports, and retains highly competent personnel.	The leader consistently recruits, trains, supports, and retains highly competent personnel.
Understands and participates in conflict management	The leader fails to understand and participate in conflict management.	The leader inconsistently understands and participates in conflict management.	The leader understands and participates in conflict management.	The leader always understands and participates in conflict management and supports a process and procedure to address issues.
Demands fidelity to the evaluation process in accordance with roles	The leader fails to demand fidelity to the evaluation process in accordance with roles.	The leader inconsistently demands fidelity to the evaluation process in accordance with roles.	The leader demands fidelity to the evaluation process in accordance with roles.	The leader consistently demands fidelity to the evaluation process in accordance with roles.
Supervises subordinates applicably	The leader fails to supervise subordinates applicably.	The leader inconsistently supervises subordinates applicably.	The leader supervises subordinates applicably.	The leader consistently supervises subordinates applicably and searches for ways to improve the quality of the evaluation program.

©Strike (2016).

Component 4b—Reports Accurately and in a Timely Manner

Rationale and Explanation
Educational leaders have a lot of data available. Local data includes enrollment, attendance, dropout and graduation rates, demographics, special education enrollment, English as a second language enrollment, AP enrollment, extracurricular activities, and tutoring. State data includes report cards, district/school progress, reporting on assessments, and ratings. Federal data includes free and reduced lunch, title monies, and other funding allocations. With a plethora of data and reports, it is imperative that educational leaders report in a timely and accurate manner. Further, data and reports must be compiled and shared in a way that is easy for the layman to view, interpret, and question.

Demonstration
Different committee and board members may exhibit, interpret, or internalize information in different ways. Just as students have different learning styles, adults receive and process information in different ways. Membership changes, so discuss with the chairs or president the most desirable way to receive information. Explain education jargon in layman's terms.

Component 4c—Upholds Rules and Regulations

Rationale and Explanation
Depending on the role, educational leaders may or may not have a voice in the development of local policy and procedures. Depending on the structure of the district or school, those developing the policies, rules, and regulations may or may not have a realistic understanding of the daily workings of a school. Regardless of our emotional reaction to or professional opinion of the rules and regulations, leaders must support and uphold all local, state, and federal policies, rules, and regulations.

In addition, the leader must collect, maintain, and report all contracts, agreements, and records in all areas, including maintenance contracts, legal, collective bargaining, licensing, and copyrighting. Also included here are upholding rules and regulations associated with acceptable use and online safety.

Demonstration
Defense in upholding policy, rules, and regulations is only as good as the district/school handbook and communication to the community. The parent handbook should not only identify the policies, rules, and procedures families

Table 3.7. Component 4b: Reports accurately and in a timely manner

Element	Level of Performance			
	Unsatisfactory	Basic	Proficient	Distinguished
Establish metrics, collect and analyze data, and interpret and articulate results	The leader fails to establish metrics, collect and analyze data, and interpret and articulate results.	The leader inconsistently establishes metrics, collects and analyzes data, and interprets and articulates results.	The leader establishes metrics, collects and analyzes data, and interprets and articulates results.	The leader always establishes metrics, collects and analyzes data, and interprets and articulates results that lead to evidence for the school improvement plan.
Adheres to compliance with local, state, and federal reporting	The leader fails to adhere to compliance with local, state, and federal reporting.	The leader inconsistently adheres to compliance with local, state, and federal reporting.	The leader adheres to compliance with local, state, and federal reporting.	The leader always adheres to and models exemplary means of compliance with local, state, and federal reporting.
Explains reports to stakeholders in understandable language	The leader fails to explain reports to stakeholders in understandable language.	The leader inconsistently explains reports to stakeholders in understandable language.	The leader explains reports to stakeholders in understandable language.	The leader always produces, explains, and provides clarification to stakeholders.

©Strike (2016).

Table 3.8. Component 4c: Upholds rules and regulations

Element		Level of Performance		
	Unsatisfactory	Basic	Proficient	Distinguished
Upholds federal, state, and local laws, policies, and regulations	The leader fails to demonstrate knowledge of laws, policies, and regulations at various levels.	The leader inconsistently upholds local laws, policies, and regulations.	The leader upholds current federal, state, and local laws, policies, and regulations.	The leader always upholds federal, state, and local laws, policies, and regulations with consistency.
Applies understanding of district policy, privacy, security, acceptable use, and online safety	The leader fails to demonstrate understanding of district policy, privacy, security, acceptable use, and online safety.	The leader inconsistently applies district policy, privacy, security, acceptable use, and online safety.	The leader demonstrates understanding of district policy, privacy, security, acceptable use, and online safety.	The leader always demonstrates and applies understanding of district policy, privacy, security, acceptable use, and online safety.
Applies understanding of copyrights and intellectual property	The leader fails to apply and understand copyrights and intellectual property.	The leader inconsistently applies and understands copyrights and intellectual property.	The leader applies and understands copyrights and intellectual property.	The leader always applies and understands copyrights and intellectual property, effectively communicates, and provides training for staff.
Manages legal and contractual agreements	The leader fails to manage legal and contractual agreements	The leader inconsistently manages legal and contractual agreements.	The leader regularly manages legal and contractual agreements.	The leader effectively manages legal and contractual agreements.
Creates and maintains records	The leader does not create and/or maintain records.	The leader inconsistently creates and maintains records.	The leader regularly creates and maintains records.	The leader effectively creates and maintains the records of the school/district.
Demonstrates knowledge of collective bargaining	The leader fails to demonstrate knowledge of collective bargaining.	The leader inconsistently demonstrates knowledge of collective bargaining.	The leader demonstrates knowledge of collective bargaining.	The leader effectively demonstrates a strong understanding and knowledge of collective bargaining.

©Strike (2016).

need but also consequences if they are not followed. For example, what is plagiarism? Is it defined in the handbook? With easy access to the Internet, are students taught about filtering information and providing citations and references? Are teachers taking the time to investigate when papers, projects, or assignments are turned in (e.g., a paper that has language the child does not typically use or extensive similarities to another student's work)? Is this the first time?

Component 4d—Practices and Refines Resourcefulness

Rationale and Explanation

In a world of ongoing budget cuts and mandates, resourceful educational leaders are in more demand. A resourceful leader taps into others' time, talents, and finances. This resourcefulness has many faces, depending on the community. Partnering with businesses can bring in funds for special events and field trips; scholarship monies; service projects; or specific projects, such as the purchase of dissection tools or summer reading material. Recognition in the community for special projects, such as a playground facelift or expansion of a wing, can be appealing to a business.

Partnerships with area schools or day-care centers can increase opportunities, such as sharing a teacher between schools when neither alone can afford the opportunity to add world language, OT/PT, or speech. Working with area systems and organizations can increase parent involvement opportunities, such as jointly providing trainings, family sessions, and fun events. Tapping into community resources, such as outreach programs, banks, hospitals, fire departments, and police departments, often provides additional opportunities to students and families for little to no cost to the school or district.

Writing grants is another way to obtain funds, and local, state, and federal channels provide many opportunities. Grant writing is time consuming and challenging, but it can be rewarding. Often, the grant is very specific based on need. Although you have no guarantee a grant will be awarded based on need, applying for grants is an excellent method for obtaining funds to support the curriculum and culture of the school or district.

In addition to researching, securing, and stewarding resources, a distinguished leader analyzes how these resources affected students:

- Identify how the resources enhanced or supported the students' instructional experience.
- Identify specific ways the resources affected student learning.

Table 3.9. Component 4d: Practices and refines resourcefulness

Element	Unsatisfactory	Basic	Proficient	Distinguished
Establishes partnerships	The leader fails to establish partnerships.	The leader inconsistently establishes partnerships.	The leader consistently establishes partnerships that are beneficial to all involved parties.	The leader effectively establishes partnerships that are monitored and analyzed continually for effectiveness.
Investigates creative funding opportunities	The leader fails to investigate creative funding opportunities.	The leader inconsistently investigates creative funding opportunities.	The leader demonstrates knowledge of creative funding opportunities that directly affect the fiscal standing of the school/district.	The leader effectively identifies, executes, and analyzes the results of creative funding opportunities for the fiscal benefit of the school/district.
Uses outside resources	The leader fails to use outside resources.	The leader inconsistently uses outside resources.	The leader regularly uses outside resources and occasionally uses these resources for the benefit of the school/district.	The leader effectively uses outside resources and consistently and effectively uses them for the direct benefit of the school/district.
Aligns and evaluates fiscal, human, and material resources	The leader fails to align and evaluate fiscal, human, and material resources.	The leader inconsistently aligns and evaluates fiscal, human, and material resources.	The leader regularly aligns and evaluates fiscal, human, and material resources.	The leader effectively aligns and evaluates fiscal, human, and material resources for the direct benefit of the school/district.

Level of Performance

©Strike (2016).

- Provide smooth rollout or implementation with input from stakeholders.
- Identify the challenges, and work with stakeholders to address them.
- Obtain feedback to improve the program and course.

Demonstration
Keep the blinders off and be open to new possibilities. When a district or school has always done things one way or its own way, it doesn't mean it's the only way. Explore options, talk to community members, network, and seek both educational and fiscal value nestled in opportunities.

For example, through working with a local alderman, opportunities for participation in community projects may present themselves, such as tending community gardens, controlling invasive weeds along the riverbank, creating and painting a mural on a building, clearing the way for an outdoor educational amphitheater, or walking in the local parade. These are excellent educational opportunities for the student to exhibit appreciation and how to give back to the community in which he or she lives.

Component 4e—Manages Effectively

Rationale and Explanation
Time management is core to effective management. Scheduling, timely attendance, keeping appointments, attentiveness, preparation, and understanding prioritization are key skills. Answering correspondence and phone calls in a timely manner is necessary to establish credibility and respect.

Management of facilities and regularly scheduled maintenance are a part of effective management. Keep in mind that regular maintenance may ding a budget, but lack of attention to the point of replacement or extensive repair will dent it. Also, part of effective management is overseeing systems and processes. Unspoken expectations or systemic ways things have *always* been done out of habit or tradition may or may not meet legal requirements.

Demonstration
Overextension of your time will have a negative effect in the long run. Focus, be in the moment and attentive to the task at hand, and put the quality of work before the quantity. Completion and follow-through are imperative to your credibility.

Table 3.10. Component 4e: Manages effectively

			Level of Performance		
Element	Unsatisfactory	Basic	Proficient	Distinguished
Prioritizes time with regard to projects	The leader fails to prioritize time with regard to projects.	The leader rarely prioritizes time with regard to projects.	The leader usually prioritizes time with regard to projects.	The leader effectively prioritizes time with regard to projects.
Oversees systems and processes	The leader does not oversee systems and processes.	The leader rarely oversees systems and processes.	The leader usually oversees systems and processes.	The leader effectively oversees systems and processes.
Oversees scheduling and maintenance of the facility	The leader fails to oversee scheduling and maintenance of the facility.	The leader inconsistently oversees scheduling and maintenance of the facility.	The leader regularly oversees scheduling and maintenance of the facility.	The leader effectively oversees scheduling and maintenance of the facility.
Balances personal and professional responsibilities	The leader fails to balance personal and professional responsibilities.	The leader rarely balances personal and professional responsibilities.	The leader usually balances personal and professional responsibilities.	The leader is a model of balancing personal and professional responsibilities effectively.

©Strike (2016).

Summary

This chapter explores the leadership framework and rubrics coupled as evaluation tools for Domain 1, which focuses on *Leadership Competencies*, and Domain 4, which focuses on *Management Competencies*. We find further explanation within the narrative descriptors provided. Evaluation is a process of self-improvement, not an end. Leaders have individual strengths and weaknesses.

The evaluation tool is a framework that identifies specific characteristics and behaviors through a process that relies on open, honest reflection by the person evaluated and open, honest, and specific communication in professional dialogue with the evaluator. This ongoing process guides the person evaluated in creating professional goals and determining the evidence to demonstrate growth in the identified areas.

Case Studies

Case Study #1

Juan's role is a district-level title supervisor. He oversees title funds in excess of $30 million for a large district of 121 schools. Juan also hires, trains, and supervises teachers who deliver title services. He has more than 100 teachers and four supervisors who report to him and assist with school visits, evaluation, training, and program delivery.

The district has opted to move to instructional coaches within the next school year, leaving Juan with the task of restructuring, preparing staff as interventionists with additional professional development and training, and revisiting personnel decisions. He will work closely with the district-level special education director to make the transition to interventionists in the fall of the following school year.

Juan has several questions and concerns as he moves through the process. His funding has strict guidelines, to which he must adhere to remain in compliance, as does special education, though they are different. The teachers he has hired and trained now need to be reviewed through the lens of licensure, interest in modeling and coaching in classrooms, moving from small groups to whole classrooms, and understanding the role of an interventionist.

The special education director has a different point of view in regard to assessments given, time between assessments to establish a monitoring system, and training teachers to use data. The idea of flexible grouping is brought up in every meeting, and although Juan likes that idea, he thinks about his teachers as they operate within the dynamics of working with different groups regularly. Juan feels defeated, as if he hadn't had a voice in the decision. He is set to address his staff tomorrow at a quarterly staff meeting.

Discussion Questions for Case Study #1

1. Who identifies the components and elements for the professional discussion?
2. If the above scenario were your observation, how would your professional discussion begin?
3. What would you highlight as strengths?
4. What would you bring to light as areas of necessary improvement?
5. What type of evidence would you look for in future observations to determine growth in the identified areas of necessary improvement?

Case Study #2

Gabby is a principal in a PK–8 building of 500 students. Although mostly neighborhood students attend, she does have students who attend through school choice. Gabby oversees her school budget, but she also has a business manager, Marilyn, onsite.

Gabby is an active administrator who loves to meet with stakeholders. She attends PTO meetings and community meetings, such as Rotary and Junior League International. She invites groups, such as Junior Achievement and Adopt a Grandparent, to work directly with the students. Through this network, she has received grants for library books, upgrades to technology, and assistance with classroom field trips. One major company provided scholarships through an essay contest for four eighth-grade students to use toward their Washington, DC, trip.

Gabby requests itemized reports and knows where every penny is, but she has noticed that Marilyn has fallen behind in rectifying the books. Financial reports are almost two months behind, and Gabby has questioned Marilyn because she sees funds being transferred between accounts unnecessarily. When it comes time to apply scholarship monies toward the students' account with the tour company, Marilyn states that the funds were never designated and have been used in another capacity (general expenses).

Gabby is very concerned that she may be seeing a shell game being played with finances, and she asks for a meeting with the superintendent. The superintendent hired Marilyn, and Gabby finds out the two were childhood friends.

Discussion Questions for Case Study #2

1. Who identifies the components and elements for the professional discussion?
2. If the above scenario were your observation, how would your professional discussion begin?
3. What would you highlight as strengths?
4. What would you bring to light as areas of necessary improvement?
5. What type of evidence would you look for in future observations to determine growth in the identified areas of necessary improvement?

Self-Assessment and Reflection

Reread the two case studies, making note of specific knowledge, skills, dispositions, and practices observed in each leader. Choose three, and align those identified skills with indicators on the rubric. Note that the first case study reflects a novice administrator, the second, a veteran. Consider how this experience affects not only the placement on the rubric but also the professional conversation.

Then, do the same for yourself. If you told your story or captured your leadership journey to date, what skills would be evident? Choose three, and align those identified skills with indicators on the rubric. If an area of strength, is it consistent or situational? If an area of deficit, what might you do to address it? What resources might you need? What evidence would you use to determine growth in this area?

References

Boaz, N., & Fox, E. A. (2014, March). Change leader, change thyself. *McKinsey Quarterly*. New York, NY: McKinsey Leadership Development. Retrieved at http://www.mckinsey.com/insights/leading_in_the_21st_century/change_leader_change_thyself

Foley, E., Mishook, J., Thompson, J., Kubiak, M., Supovitz, J., & Rhude-Faust, M. (2008). *Beyond test scores: Leading indicators for education*. Providence, RI: Brown University's Annenberg Institute for School Reform.

Fullan, M. (2011). *Learning is the work*. Retrieved from https://michaelfullan.ca/wp-content/uploads/2016/06/13396087260.pdf

Garmston, R., & Wellman, B. (2013). *The adaptive school: A sourcebook for developing collaborative groups*. Lanham, MD: Rowman & Littlefield.

Goksoy, S. (2016). *Analysis of the relationship between shared leadership and distributed leadership. Eurasian Journal of Educational Research, 65,* 295–312. http://dx.doi.org/10.14689/ejer.2016.65.17

Green, R. (2016). *Practicing the art of leadership: A problem-based approach to implementing the professional standards for educational leaders.* (5th ed.). New York, NY: Pearson Education, Inc.

Hargreaves, A. (2015, February 6). *Keynote: Professional capital.* Milwaukee, WI: Wisconsin State Reading Association.

Hargreaves, A., & Fullan, M. (2008). *What's worth fighting for in the principalship?* New York, NY: Teachers College Press.

Hersey, P., & Blanchard, K. (1982). *Management of organizational behavior: Utilizing human resources.* (4th ed.). Englewood Cliffs, NJ: Prentice Hall.

Jackson, K., Fixsen, D., & Ward, C. (2018, February). *Four domains for rapid school improvement: An implementation framework.* University of North Carolina, Chapel Hill, NC: National Implementation Research Network.

Jones, S., Harvey, M., Lefoe, G., & Ryland, K. (2013). Synthesizing theory and practice: Distributed leadership in higher education. *Educational Management Administration and Leadership.* Retrieved from http://emedia.rmit.edu.au/distribute dleadership/?q=node/10

Killion, J. (2011, June). A bold move forward. *The Learning Professional, 32*(3), 10–14.

Maxwell, J., & Elmore, T. (2007). *The Maxwell leadership bible.* (2nd ed.). Nashville, TN: Maxwell Motivation, Inc.

Miller, W. (2011). *Building on what we've learned: Report 2011.* New York, NY: Wallace Foundation.

National Association of Secondary School Principals (NASSP) and National Association of Elementary School Principals (NAESP). (2013). *Leadership matters.* Reston and Alexandria, VA: NASSP and NAESP.

Sergiovanni, T. (1992). *Moral leadership: Getting to the heart of school improvement.* San Francisco, CA: John Wiley and Sons.

Yukl, G., & Gardner, W., III. (2020). *Leadership in organizations.* (9th ed.). Boston, MA: Pearson Education, Inc.

~

CHAPTER FOUR

Examination of Effective Leadership

Management is doing things right; leadership is doing the right things.

—Peter Drucker (2012)

Objectives

At the conclusion of this chapter you will be able to:

1. Articulate the historical context of effective leadership (PSEL 1, 2, 3, 4, 5, 6, 7, 8, 9, 10; NELP 1, 2, 3, 4, 5, 6, 7, 8).
2. Articulate personal traits and abilities and a willingness to develop further traits in order to become an effective leader (PSEL 1, 2, 3, 4, 5, 6, 7, 8, 9, 10; NELP 1, 2, 3, 4, 5, 6, 7, 8).
3. Distinguish effective leadership behaviors and responsibilities that one has as a school leader (PSEL 1, 2, 3, 4, 5, 6, 7, 8, 9, 10; NELP 1, 2, 3, 4, 5, 6, 7, 8).
4. Design a platform of effective leadership traits, behaviors, responsibilities, and theories for use in schools and districts as current and future leaders (PSEL 1, 2, 3, 4, 5, 6, 7, 8, 9, 10; NELP 1, 2, 3, 4, 5, 6, 7, 8).

A Look at Leadership

We experience leadership throughout various levels (e.g., international, national, state, and local) as well as sectors (e.g., public, private, parochial, charter, choice, and for profit) and types of organizations (e.g., business, education, health care, and church). Who are the most effective leaders? What is it that they do and say that makes them successful? Who are the least effective leaders? What is it that they do and say that makes them unsuccessful?

We all make judgments about leaders. These assessments are based on a set of criteria. In evaluating school leaders, we come with our expectations of what qualities they should have (e.g., visionary and dedicated), behaviors they should exhibit in daily practice (e.g., visibility in the building), and theories they should practice (e.g., servant and instructional leadership). We also come with our dreams, hopes, failures, and experiences. Depending on these positive and negative experiences of leadership, we develop a sense of the concept of leadership. For those who are leaders and those who plan to assume leadership positions, it is important to know how the thinking on leadership has evolved over the years.

Leadership Traits

In Table 4.1, a historical overview of research on effective leadership begins with *trait theories*. Successful leaders seem to have certain abilities that empower them to be effective as leaders.

Table 4.1. Trait Theories

Years	Theorists	Findings
1948	Stogdill	Some people may be born with qualities that make them successful leaders.
1992–2001	Nanus (1992) Maxwell (1995) Collins (2001) Buckingham and Clifton (2001)	There are traits that successful/effective leaders have in common.
2008	ISLLC Standards	Six personal qualities of effective leaders.
2011	Smoker	Focus.
2012	Northouse	Six key traits for successful leaders.
	Siccone	Five essential skills for successful school leadership.

The first studies on effective leadership focused on traits. The term *traits* refers to those qualities, gifts, or unique characteristics that leaders seem to have that make a difference in how they lead organizations. Examples of traits include courage, intelligence, determination, and communication skills. Theorists, such as Stogdill (1948), were addressing the following questions: What traits do you need to be an effective leader? Can leaders learn these traits? Can we distinguish successful leaders from unsuccessful leaders based on the traits they were gifted with from birth?

Nanus (1992) and Maxwell (1995) suggested that effective leaders were *passionate, self-confident,* and *flexible.* Collins (2001) presented Level 5 leaders as successful leaders who were *humble, driven,* and *professional.* He distinguished between good companies and great companies by emphasizing the impact of Level 5 leaders. They relied on high standards, surrounded themselves with the right people, created a culture of high discipline, honestly looked at the facts regarding their companies, and entertained difficult questions.

In 2001, Buckingham and Clifton identified 34 signature talents or strengths that effective leaders share. The researchers suggested that each person is strong in a few of these talents and weak in a few others. Effective leaders need to select the right people, make decisions, focus on training of leaders, and be careful about promoting people based on their strengths.

The ISLLC (Interstate School Leaders Licensure Consortium) standards (2008) asserted that successful effective leaders were focused on vision; school culture and instructional program; operations, management, and resources; collaboration with families and community; ethics; and political, social, legal, and cultural contexts. Created by the Council of Chief State School Officers (CCSSO), the ISLLC standards provided a common set of standards for all states to be used by all practicing leaders and for those preparing to be leaders.

Updated in 2015, the ISLLC standards are now known as the PSEL (Professional Standards for Educational Leaders). Successful leaders need to address the mission, vision, and core values; ethics and professional norms; equity and cultural responsiveness; curriculum, instruction, and assessment; community of care and support for students; professional capacity of school personnel; professional community for teachers and staff; operations and management; and school improvement. More on the PSEL will be addressed in chapter 5.

Smoker (2011) insisted that effective school leaders *focus* on the essentials to ensure that every student receives a quality education. Instead of adopting fads, programs, and new innovations, Smoker asserted that schools create a decent curriculum; provide excellent lessons; and offer lots of reading, writing, and discussion. Once schools focus on these essentials, the impact helps to reform learning.

Northouse (2012) posited six key traits for effective leaders: *intelligence, confidence, charisma, determination, sociability,* and *integrity. Intelligence* means having good language skills, perceptual skills, and reasoning ability. *Confidence* refers to leaders who feel secure about themselves and what they can accomplish. *Charisma* is the special appeal that leaders have to inspire and motivate others. *Determination,* for the leader, involves getting the job done. Building relationships with others is the *sociability* element of successful leadership. Honesty with self and others is the sixth trait, referred to as *integrity.*

Siccone (2012) wrote that effective school leaders share five essential sets of skills:

1. *Confidence.* Leaders believe in themselves and inspire others.
2. *Communication.* Leaders are effective communicators with clear articulation and shared meanings.
3. *Collaboration.* Leaders work with others to set goals, plan strategies, and solve problems.
4. *Coaching.* Leaders work in teams.
5. *Continuous improvement.* Leaders see change as an opportunity for growth.

In *The Challenge for School Leaders* (2015), Ron Warwick concludes that effective leaders demonstrate common traits and abilities that add value to any organization of which they are a part. Four general traits of effective leaders are sees clearly, is a team player, offers genuine support, and relies on statistical data (pp. 125–126).

Leadership Behaviors

The contributions of trait theorists invite school leaders and future leaders to do a personal inventory concerning what traits they already have and what traits they may need to acquire at greater depth. While traits are indeed gifts and qualities we have as effective leaders, we also need to go further in our study on effective leadership by addressing leadership behaviors.

These are the factors that leaders need to do and say to be effective in the schools they lead. The key question became, What types of behaviors do effective leaders practice? A number of *leadership styles* emerged. See Table 4.2 for an overview of leadership behaviors.

Table 4.2. Leadership Behaviors

Years	Theorists	Leadership Style
1939	Lewin, Lippett, & White	Autocratic Democratic Laissez-faire
1957	Stogdill & Coons	Initiating structure Consideration
1961, 1967	Likert	Exploitive authoritative Benevolent authoritative Consultative Participative
1960	McGregor	Theory X Theory Y
1982	Hersey & Blanchard	Situational leadership Four leadership styles: Telling, participating, selling, and delegating
1989	Stephen Covey	The 7 Habits of Highly Effective People
2003, 2005	Cotton (2003) Marzano, Waters, & McNulty (2005)	25 Categories of principal behavior 21 Responsibilities of the school leader
2003	Harvey, Cottrell, & Lucia	The Leadership Secrets of Santa Claus
2008	Cockerel	Creating Magic
2009	Scharmer	Theory U: Seven effective leadership behaviors to overcome adverse situations

Lewin, Lippitt, and White (1939), at the University of Iowa, identified three leadership behaviors that could be examples of effective leadership. *Autocratic* leaders made decisions, gave directions, and managed followers. *Democratic* leaders, on the other hand, invited shared decision-making and encouraged a sense of community. *Laissez-faire* leaders, in contrast, gave no directions and allowed followers complete authority. They found that followers preferred democratic leaders, were dissatisfied with autocratic and laissez-faire leaders, and could be most productive with autocratic and democratic leaders.

In 1957 at the Ohio State University, Stogdill and Coons studied effective leadership behavior from the perspective of initiating structure and consideration. *Initiating structure* involved leaders who set performance standards, work deadlines, and scheduling. *Consideration* was a term applied to leaders who focused on relationships, mutual trust and respect, consultation, and warmth. The results showed that leaders high on both initiating structure and consideration were considered the most effective.

At the University of Michigan, Likert (1961 and 1967) identified four types of leadership behavior that could be effective. *Exploitive authoritative* leaders were hierarchical and made all decisions in a system where followers were not trusted. *Benevolent authoritative* leaders operated in a master–servant system whereby the leader did involve the followers to some extent but not much. *Consultative* leaders asked employees for input, but the final decision was still with the leader. *Participative* leaders trusted followers and involved them in decision-making in a system that had good communication. Participative leaders were viewed most effective by employees, and their work production increased.

Theorist Douglas McGregor (1960) asserted that what a leader believed about human beings affected their leadership behavior. In *Theory X*, McGregor said that some leaders did not trust their workers and therefore were in control of everything. They would *expect* and *inspect*. *Theory Y*, on the other hand, suggested that leaders trusted people and sought collaboration in decision-making. Most followers preferred Theory Y leaders and insisted they were more effective than Theory X leaders.

Scharmer (2009) took up the idea of theory and presented a change management process to help leaders overcome past difficulties and failures. This was called *Theory U*. Seven effective leadership behaviors exhibited by collaborative teams can help organizations become successful. These leadership behaviors are *listening, observing, sensing, presencing, crystallizing, prototyping,* and *performing*.

Paul Hersey and Kenneth Blanchard (1982) added another perspective to what effective leadership might look like. In the *situational leadership theory*, the authors suggested that effective leaders adjust their leadership style and behavior to the experience and expertise of followers. An effective leader knows each follower and when to apply each of these styles.

Four leadership styles emerged:

- *Telling style*. When followers cannot do and are unwilling to do the task, the leader takes over.
- *Participating style*. When followers cannot do the task but are willing to do the task, the leader provides guidance.
- *Selling style*. When followers can do the task but are unwilling to do the task, the leader has to persuade them to do the task.
- *Delegating style*. When followers can do the task and are willing to do the task, the leader empowers the followers to do what they need to do.

Stephen Covey (1989) also added to the discussion on effective leadership when he wrote his very popular book, *The 7 Habits of Highly Effective People*. In the book, he posits seven behaviors or directives: be proactive; begin with the end in mind; put first things first; think win-win; seek first to understand, then to be understood; synergize; and sharpen the saw.

Effective school leadership behaviors were most clearly articulated in the research work of Cotton (2003) and Marzano, Waters, and McNulty (2005). Cotton discovered 25 areas of principal behavior that positively affected student achievement, attitudes, behavior, and dropout rates as well as teacher attitudes and behaviors. Her conclusion was that principal leadership has an indirect effect on student outcomes.

Marzano et al. (2005) identified and defined 21 responsibilities of principal leadership that correlate with student achievement. Two key questions were addressed in their book: (1) To what extent does leadership play a role in whether a school is effective or ineffective? (2) How much of a school's impact on student achievement is due to the leadership of the principal? Results indicated that there was a statistically significant relationship between each of the principal's responsibilities and student achievement. This is an important addition to the research on effective leadership.

In Table 4.3, the 25 principal behaviors and 21 responsibilities of the school leader are listed but not compared. A comparison of the two can be found in the Marzano et al.'s (2005) book, *School Leadership That Works* (pp. 178–179.) The list of principal behaviors and responsibilities of school leaders is quite similar. They differ in that Cotton (2003) did not quantitatively estimate the effect of principal leadership on student achievement.

Marzano and Waters (2009) and Marzano et al. (2005) also asserted that the relationship between principal leadership and student achievement was indirect rather than direct. Principals do not teach students. Teachers provided instruction to students. The principals influenced teachers who had a direct influence on students. As such, the principal's effect on student achievement passed through teachers.

Another insight from Marzano et al. (2005) was that two factors come with the 21 responsibilities of the school leader. These factors were first-order and second-order change. *First-order change* was incremental and involved the daily behaviors (the 21 responsibilities) that a school leader must do for the operation of the school. *Second-order change* was a dramatic departure from the usual way of doing things and focused on seven of those responsibilities (*knowledge of curriculum, instruction and assessment, optimizer, intellectual stimulation, change agent, monitoring and evaluating, flexibility, and ideals/beliefs*).

Table 4.3. Twenty-Five Principal Behaviors and 21 Responsibilities of School Leaders

25 Categories of Principal Behavior (Cotton, 2003)	21 Responsibilities of the School Leader (Marzano, Waters, & McNulty, 2005)
1. Safe and orderly environment	1. Affirmation
2. Vision and goals focused on high levels of student learning	2. Change Agent
3. High expectations for student learning	3. Contingent Rewards
4. Self-confidence, responsibility, and perseverance	4. Communication
5. Visibility and accessibility	5. Culture
6. Positive and supportive climate	6. Discipline
7. Communication and interaction	7. Flexibility
8. Emotional and interpersonal support	8. Focus
9. Parent and community outreach and involvement	9. Ideals/Beliefs
10. Rituals, ceremonies, and other symbolic actions	10. Input
11. Shared leadership, decision making, and staff empowerment	11. Intellectual Stimulation
12. Collaboration	12. Involvement in Curriculum, Instruction, and Assessment
13. Instructional leadership	13. Knowledge of Curriculum, Instruction, and Assessment
14. Ongoing pursuit of high levels of student learning	14. Monitoring/Evaluating
15. Norm of continuous improvement	15. Optimizer
16. Discussion of instructional issues	16. Order
17. Classroom observation and feedback to teachers	17. Outreach
18. Support of teachers' autonomy	18. Relationships
19. Support of risk taking	19. Resources
20. Professional development opportunities and resources	20. Situational Awareness
21. Protecting instructional time	21. Visibility
22. Monitoring student progress and sharing findings	
23. Use of student progress for program improvement	
24. Recognition of student and staff achievement	
25. Role modeling	

The Leadership Secrets of Santa Claus by Harvey, Cottrell, and Lucia (2003) added a humorous interpretation of effective leadership behaviors for the readers to consider. The eight behaviors were *build a wonderful workshop, choose the reindeer wisely, make a list and check it twice, listen to the elves, get beyond the red wagons, share the milk and cookies, find out who has been naughty and nice,* and *be good for goodness sake.*

A unique contribution to the study of leadership behaviors came from the Disney Corporation. Lee Cockerell (2008), the executive vice president of operations at Walt Disney World for 10 years, added 10 commonsense leadership strategies from a life at Disney. His strategies included *remember everyone is important, break the mold, make your people your brand, create magic through training, eliminate hassles, learn the truth, burn the free fuel, stay ahead of the pack, be careful about what you say and do*, and *develop character*.

Warwick (2015) provided a summary to understand effective leadership thinking and action. He asserted 10 concepts and values:

1. Commit to a common purpose.
2. Every person is of equal value.
3. Good decisions are based on good information and collaborative analysis of this information.
4. We are human and make mistakes.
5. Professional development is essential to improvement and is forever ongoing.
6. Higher cognitive processes are taught and do not automatically develop when one grows older.
7. Foster a joy of learning: Remove the fear of offering new ways of thinking and problem solving.
8. Be a team player.
9. Leaders are accountable for the process and performance of the system they are leading.
10. Aim to leave things better than when we entered! (pp. 126–127)

A new contribution to the study of leadership traits and behaviors comes in the publication of this book. The authors believe that *The Leadership Framework* is a practical resource for both leaders and evaluators as they address what constitutes effective leadership. The four domains that constitute traits and behaviors identified are *leadership competencies, professional learning and growth, instructional practices*, and *management competencies*. Key leadership theories serve as a foundation for these domains.

Leadership Theories

Through examination of leadership theories and the theorists behind them, we further and deepen our understanding of effective leadership. After analyzing multiple theories, threads and commonalities became evident. It is these common traits in which we anchor beliefs and move from theory to practice. Our study examined *transactional, transformational, instructional, high impact instructional, distributed, servant, moral, spiritual,* and *uplifting leadership theories*. See Table 4.4 for an overview of the theories.

Table 4.4. Leadership Theories

Theory, Theorists, and Date	Focus of Theory
Transactional leadership Burns, 1978	Give-and-take exchange
Transformational leadership Burns, 1978	Personal and organizational change
Instructional leadership Blasé & Blasé, 1999, and others	Student learning and instructional methods
High impact leadership Hattie, 2015	What does high impact mean in learning?
Distributive leadership Elmore, 2000; Spillane & Scherer, 2004	Leadership is not a one-man or one-woman job.
Servant leadership Greenleaf, 1977; Spears, 1995	Leadership is serving others.
Moral leadership Sergiovanni, 1992	Balancing the head, heart, and hand
Spiritual leadership Fry & Nisiewicz, 2013	Balancing the head, heart, hand, and spirit
Uplifting leadership Hargreaves & Boyle, 2015	Raising spirits, hopes, and performances of all

James Burns (1978) began the discussion on effective leadership by introducing the terms *transactional* and *transformational leadership* to the business and education communities. Transactional leadership is a trading of one thing for another between the leader and follower. Effective school leaders have goals and objectives to meet (teaching responsibilities for teachers, outcomes for students) for the school, while teachers and students have needs and desires (money, self-efficacy, promotions, and what they should know and be able to do) that they seek. There is a social exchange and mutual satisfaction.

Transformational leadership, built on transactional leadership, is about change. Inspiring school leaders motivate teachers and students to go beyond their personal interests to focus on the greater good of the school. Mutual relationships develop between the school leaders, teachers, and students, and these relationships are deepened by common values, vision, mission, and goals. This process of coming together has a transforming effect on all stakeholders. This is the second theory of effective leadership.

Bass (1985) distinguished the roles of effective transformational leaders as the "Four I's": *individual consideration, intellectual stimulation, inspirational motivation*, and *idealized influence*. Bass and Avolio (1994) and Leithwood (1994) adapted the Four I's of transformational leadership to education. The Four I's are four behaviors that effective school leaders should do and be and, as a result, will affect teachers and students so much that they become transformed. Table 4.5 provides a graphic example of each of the Four I's.

Table 4.5. The Four I's of Transformational Leadership

The Four I's	School Leader Example
Individual consideration	Differentiation
Intellectual stimulation	Professional learning
Inspiration motivation	Responds to neediest students
Idealized influence	Modeling

An example of *individual consideration* is when a school leader realizes that not all the teachers are the same. The school leader works with the new teacher in a different way than what he or she might work with a veteran teacher. There is differentiation in the approach based on expertise and experience.

Intellectual stimulation happens when the school leader invites teachers to learn and apply new teaching methods. An example of this is when the school leader and teachers engage in a three-year book study to understand and use the nine instructional strategies presented in the book *Classroom Instruction That Works* (Dean, Hubble, Pitler, & Stone, 2012).

When teachers see the school leader present in classrooms in daily walk-throughs and at extracurricular activities after school, the teachers are given an example of *inspirational motivation*. Even more so, teachers are inspired by the school leader when they see the leader working to establish a school-wide diversity program that values each person for who he or she is.

School leaders are role models for teachers and students. When the teachers and students see the school leader as respectful, caring, personal, and a lifelong learner, the school leader provides an example of *idealized influence*. By what they say and more so by what they do, school leaders help establish the climate and culture of the local school.

A third effective leadership theory is *instructional leadership*. There has been a new focus on the school leader as an instructional leader as politicians and the general public have demanded higher academic standards and more accountability from schools. The struggle for school leaders has been to balance their roles and time as manager–administrators and instructional leaders. Consider how this plays in to your current placement and role.

A further struggle has been in being able to define what we mean by instructional leadership. Reflect momentarily on your definition of instructional leadership. Table 4.6 presents some of the functions of effective instructional leadership. These functions influence how one both defines and perceives effective instructional leadership. Notice the similarities and differences. Evaluate yourself as an effective instructional leader against these models.

Table 4.6. Models of Instructional Leadership

Theorists and Year	Functions of Instructional Leaders
Hallinger, Murphy, Well, Mesa & Mitman 1983	1. Define the school's mission 2. Manage curriculum, instruction 3. Promote a positive school culture
Smith & Andrews 1989	1. Resource provider 2. Instructional resource 3. Communicator 4. Visible presence

The research of Marks and Printy (2003) concluded that, when transformational and instructional leadership coexist in leadership, the impact on student performance is significant. Separately, each of these leadership styles can make a difference with students, but a bigger impact comes from the two leadership styles combined. Table 4.7 illustrates the characteristics of each leadership style.

Robinson, Lloyd, and Rowe (2008) compared transformational leaders to instructional leaders. Their findings suggest that transformational leaders focus on teachers, set a vision for the school, create common goals, set directions, and give teachers a lot of autonomy. The overall effect of transformational leaders was .11, while the instructional leaders overall effect was .42. Instructional leaders, on the other hand, focus more on students, student learning, and instructional issues. This is a big difference in the effect.

Table 4.7. Characteristics of Transformational and Instructional Leadership Styles

Transformational Leadership	Instructional Leadership
Introduce innovation	Improve professional practice
Shape cultures	Interact around curriculum and instructional reform efforts
Transform school culture	Coordinate curriculum
Make teachers partners in decision-making	Supervise classroom instruction
Practice problem finding/problem solving	Facilitate teacher growth
Stress goals of improving organizational performance	Involve teachers in sustained dialogue and decision-making about educational matters
Collaborate with stakeholders	Include teachers as equal partners
Increase commitment	Acknowledge teacher professionalism
Articulate the larger good	Capitalize on teacher knowledge and skill
Develop followers	Share instructional leadership
Focus on mission, performance, and culture	Seek out ideas, insight, and expertise of teachers
	Set high expectations
	Monitor student progress
	Create communities of learners

Source: Cordeiro, P., & Cunningham, W. (2013).

John Hattie (2015) referred to this difference as *high impact instructional leadership*, which begins with what effective leaders think their job is in the school. This is the fourth theory of effective leadership. Seven major mind frames inform these effective leaders:

1. Understand the need to focus on learning and the impact of teaching.
2. Believe that their fundamental task is to evaluate the effect of everyone in their school on student learning.
3. Believe that success and failure in student learning is about what they, as teachers or leaders, did or didn't do. They see themselves as change agents.
4. See assessment as feedback on their impact.
5. Understand the importance of dialogue and listening to student and teacher voice.
6. Set challenging targets for themselves and for teachers to maximize student outcomes.
7. Welcome errors, share what they've learned from their own errors, and create environments in which teachers and students can learn from errors without losing face.

Hattie, Masters, and Birch (in press) define impact by asking four questions. Is the impact valid? Parents, students, teachers, and leaders agree on the outcomes to focus on, and these might include gains in achievement, increased attendance, and evidence that students moved to deeper learning. Is the impact equitable? All students must be affected. How great an impact are you seeking to achieve? This is expressed in improvements observed in student work samples over time. What teacher practices are most related to student learning? Teaching practices need to be examined in terms of evidence of their impact on student learning.

DuFour and Marzano (2011) identified two of the barriers that effective school leaders face. First, isolated teachers were difficult to reach. Second, no one leader had the time, energy, skills, or knowledge to fulfill every one of the 21 responsibilities of school leaders identified in the Marzano et al. (2005) book, *School Leadership That Works*.

The response of DuFour and Marzano (2011) to these two barriers was to implement *professional learning communities* (PLCs) *and collaborative teams*. According to DuFour, DuFour, Eaker, and Many (2010, p. 11), a PLC can be defined this way: "The PLC concept represents '*an ongoing process* in which educators work collaboratively in recurring cycles of collective inquiry and action research to achieve better results for the students they serve.'"

Through the PLC process and collaborative teams, principals have a venue to address 19 of the 21 responsibilities identified by Marzano et al. (2005). Only two of the responsibilities (contingent rewards and discipline) are focused on individuals. The other responsibilities can be achieved in the team process, which leads to the possibility of shared leadership.

Shared leadership recognizes the fact that effective leadership is not a one-man or one-woman job. Shared leadership is also called *collaborative leadership* or *distributed leadership*. This is the fifth theory of effective leadership. Elmore (2000) and Spillane and Sherer (2004) focused on leadership that shares responsibilities with others. Leadership involves participation, empowerment, dialogue, and cooperation of a team or group of leaders. This might be the district level team, the building level team, teacher leaders, department chairpersons, or grade level leaders. Consider how this theory is reflected in your setting.

A sixth theory of effective leadership comes from the research findings of Greenleaf (1977) and Spears (1995), who coined the term *servant leadership* in which the leader desires to serve the needs of others and not their own. The characteristics of servant leadership are *calling, listening, empathy, healing awareness, persuasion, conceptualization, foresight, stewardship, growth,* and *building community.* Consider how servant leadership is exhibited in your district and by whom.

The seventh theory of effective leadership is *moral leadership.* Sergiovanni (1992) suggested that effective leaders will do the right thing for their students, teachers, and parents when they balance the head, the heart, and the hand. The head refers to our thoughts and mindscapes. The heart deals with our emotions and feelings. The hand is our actions and what we do. Effective leaders are moral leaders.

An eighth theory of effective leadership that is being considered today is *spiritual leadership.* Fry and Nisiewicz (2013) suggest that spiritual leadership adds to the existing theories in which some components may be missing. Spiritual leadership is a holistic blend of the mind, the body, the heart, and the spirit. Practices of spiritual leadership include *inner life, satisfaction with life, membership, meaning and calling, altruistic love, hope and faith, vision, organizational commitment,* and *productivity.*

Hargreaves and Boyle (2015) concluded in their research that effective leadership that is concerned should be called *uplifting leadership.* This ninth theory of leadership is about being consistent in what we lead, why we lead, and how we lead. Uplifting leadership raises the spirits, hopes, and performances of all people in the school community by our words and actions.

The research of Hargreaves and Boyle (2015) identified six critical factors of uplifting leadership that are paradoxical combinations of opposites: *counterintuitive thinking combined with disciplined application, dreaming with determination, collaboration with competition, metrics with meaning, pushing and pulling people into change,* and *long-term sustainability with short-term success.*

Thus far, we have examined traits, behaviors, and theories to understand what we mean by the term *effective leadership.* Hopefully, each of these factors has helped you to determine your own sense of effective leadership by comparing your everyday practices with this wisdom from the work of researchers. In the following, we move on to the key qualities of effective leadership.

Key Qualities of Effective Leadership

Leithwood and Riehl (2003) asserted that effective leaders mobilize and work with others to achieve shared goals. Important qualities that emerged from this finding were that effective leaders worked with others to create a shared purpose and direction, empowered others to be effective, and performed a set of functions and roles that were shared by many people. Effective leaders provided direction and exercised influence.

A major finding from the research of Leithwood and Riehl (2003) was that there was a core set of leadership practices that form the basis of what they called successful or effective leadership. Three broad categories included competencies, orientations, and considerations. They are *setting direction, developing people,* and *developing the organization.*

Setting direction involved identifying and articulating a vision, creating shared meanings, creating high performance expectations, fostering the acceptance of group goals, monitoring organizational performance, and communicating. This dimension of leadership was focused on goals and vision. As a result, the school leaders have a direct influence on all members of the school community.

Developing people was influencing the human resources in schools. Elements of this category included offering intellectual stimulation, providing individualized support, and providing an appropriate model. This dimension of leadership was focused on the work of people in schools and how the leader can give direction by influencing the teachers in how they instructed the students. As a result, school leaders have an indirect influence upon students.

Developing the organization was the work of school leaders to empower the whole school to become a professional learning community. Elements of this category included strengthening school culture, modifying the organizational structure, building collaborative processes, and managing the environment. As a result, school leaders have a direct influence not only on all members of the school community but also with the larger community in which the school exists.

In *Rethinking Leadership*, Sergiovanni (1999) presented a hierarchy of five tiers or qualities of leadership that must be considered. At the base was the *technical leader* (tier one), who ensured that all systems of the school were on track to where they should be. The *human leader* (tier two) took care of the relationships between people to ensure that everyone was doing what they should be doing. The *educational leader* (tier three) focused on curriculum, instruction, assessment, and professional learning for teachers and on increased learning for students.

Sergiovanni (1999) insisted that, for school leaders to be effective, they needed to be proficient in each of these three tiers of leadership in ascending order. Not being proficient in any of these areas resulted in the ineffectiveness of the school leader. But these three areas of leadership were not enough to become excellent leaders. Two other areas were needed to achieve excellence.

Symbolic leaders (tier four) reminded people of what was most important in the school community and helped them to develop a vision that was communicated to all in a shared sense of purpose. *Cultural leaders* (tier five, the highest level of excellence) added to the vision and sense of purpose by including a mission ideology that inspired people to become more motivated and involved in the school with a common spirit. See Table 4.8 for a better understanding of rethinking leadership.

Table 4.8.   Rethinking Leadership

Tiers of Leadership	Degree of Excellence
5. Cultural leaders	1. Mission and common spirit
4. Symbolic leaders	2. Values and vision
3. Educational leaders	3. Teaching and learning
2. Human leaders	4. Human resources
1. Technical leaders	5. Management of all systems

Source: Sergiovanni (1999).

These core practices of effective school leaders and tiers of excellent leaders provide core qualities for school leaders to consider and implement in their own school settings. In each of these categories, one can see the influence of the professional standards. The categories can also be cross-referenced with *The Framework for Effective Leadership* and its four domains of leadership competencies, professional learning and growth, student learning, and management competencies. There are many common qualities that emerge to help practicing leaders and potential leaders to consider as they reflect on effective leadership.

Four Themes from the Leadership Theories

Based on our examination of leadership theories in this chapter, four themes emerged:

- Trait theories
- Behavioral theories
- Situational leader theories
- Relationship leader theories

The *trait theories* focused on the personal characteristics of effective leaders. Stogdill (1974) distinguished these qualities as traits and skills. Examples of traits of effective leaders were assertive, dependable, and self-confident.

Skills of effective leaders were creative, persuasive, diplomatic, and socially skilled.

The *behavioral theories* specified the actions of effective leaders. Lewin, Lippitt, and White (1939) described three types of leadership styles that might be effective: autocratic, democratic, and laissez-faire. Initiating structure with a focus on tasks and personal consideration of people were two types of behavior for effective leaders in the research of Stogdill and Coons (1957).

Cotton (2003) examined 25 categories of principal behavior (e.g., visibility and accessibility), while Marzano et al. (2005) asserted that 21 responsibilities (e.g., flexibility and intellectual stimulation) of the school leader can affect student learning and effect second-order change. Leithwood and Riehl (2003) articulated three main activities for effective school leaders: setting directions, developing people, and developing the organization.

The *situational leader theories* insisted that effective leaders adjusted their style to the experience and expertise of the followers. Hersey and Blanchard (1982) called this *situational leadership*. One type of leadership does not work for all teachers. An effective leader knows each teacher and how to work with him or her. This is like the effective teachers who know how to differentiate teaching and thus affect learning for every student.

The *relationship leader theories* documented multiple examples of effective leaders that built networks with followers. Examples of these leadership theories included *transactional and transformational leadership* from the research of Burns (1978), in which there is an exchange of services and benefits between the leader and followers.

These four themes from our examination of leadership theories can be seen in Table 4.9. The leadership theories are the foundation for building the standards that provide an outline for what effective leaders should know and be able to do. The PSEL for effective leadership are used in most states. In chapter 5, we will link the theories to the PSEL and *The Leadership Framework*.

Table 4.9. Four Themes in the Leadership Theories

Trait theories	Leadership depends on the unique characteristics of the individual.
Behavior theories	Leadership style is demonstrated in what the leader does or does not do.
Situational theories	Leadership actions depend on the expertise and experience of followers.
Relationship theories	Leadership is not a one-man or one-woman job.

Summary

The purpose of this chapter was to examine effective leadership. Traits are abilities that many leaders seem to have naturally or need to learn. Behaviors are the practices put into action by the leader. Theories are the models that help explain practice and theory. The key qualities of leadership are foundational traits, behaviors, and theories of effective leadership. Each of these elements examined in this chapter is meant to be an invitation for practicing and future leaders to distinguish effective leadership behaviors and responsibilities that one has as a school leader and continue to grow. The research serves as building blocks for our understanding of *The Leadership Framework*.

Case Study

You are invited to interview for the superintendent position in the Selkirk Unified School District. The interview committee asks you to present your opening statements to the leaders, teachers, and staff of the district. In a 20-minute talk, articulate your traits (gifts), your leadership style, the leadership theories that resonate with who you are, and the challenges you expect to address as the new leader of the Selkirk Unified School District.

Discussion Questions for Case Study

1. Create a personal inventory of your traits (gifts) for leadership. What traits do you have, and what traits do you need to be an effective leader?
2. In the behavioral leadership studies, Lewin, Lippitt, and White (1939) identified three leadership behaviors: autocratic, democratic, and laissez-faire. Conduct a discussion on the strengths and weaknesses of each of these leadership styles. In what situations would these styles be effective or not effective?
3. In reading over the 25 categories of principal behaviors (Cotton, 2003) and the 21 responsibilities of a school leader (Marzano et al., 2005), in which categories/responsibilities are you proficient? In which ones do you need to improve? Which ones are more important for you to do at this time at your school? Why? Discuss these issues with your classmates and/or fellow school leaders.

4. Nine theories of leadership were examined. Which theories are meaningful to you? Are there other theories not mentioned here that speak to your leadership experience? If so, what are they? Share your answers with others.

Self-Assessment and Reflection

Leithwood and Riehl (2003) identified three core practices for effective leaders. They are setting directions, developing people, and developing the organization. Reflect on your experience as a leader. Critique yourself and consider examples of each of these categories that support your critique. Consider your level and experience of leadership (veteran, novice, or preparing for future roles). In which practices are you proficient, and in which ones do you believe you need improvement or more experience? Were there theories presented in this chapter that have more meaning to you than others? Explain why?

References

Bass, B. (1985). *Leadership and performance beyond expectations*. New York, NY: Free Press.

Bass, B., & Avolio, B. (1994). *Improving organizational effectiveness through transformational leadership*. Thousand Oaks, CA: Sage.

Buckingham, M., & Clifton, D. (2001). *Now, discover your strengths*. New York, NY: Free Press.

Burns, J. (1978). *Leadership*. New York, NY: Harper & Row.

Cockerell, L. (2008). *Creating magic: 10 common sense leadership strategies from a life at Disney*. New York, NY: Doubleday.

Collins, J. (2001). *Good to great: Why some companies make the leap . . . and others don't*. New York, NY: HarperCollins.

Cordeiro, P., & Cunningham, W. (2013). *Educational leadership: A bridge to improved practice*. (5th ed.). New York, NY: Pearson.

Cotton, K. (2003). *Principals and student achievement: What the research says*. Alexandria, VA: Association for Supervision and Curriculum Development.

Covey, S. (1989). *The 7 habits of highly effective people: Powerful lessons in personal change*. New York, NY: Simon & Schuster.

Dean, C., Hubble, E., Pitler, H., & Stone, B. (2012). *Classroom instruction that works*. (2nd ed.). Denver, CO: McREL.

Drucker, P. (2012). *Leadership insights from Peter Drucker*. Retrieved from https://leadershipdynamics.wordpress.com/2012/02/22/leadership-insights-from-peter-drucker/

DuFour, R., Dufour, R., Eaker, R., & Many, T. (2010). *Learning by doing: A handbook for professional learning communities at work.* (2nd ed.). Bloomington, IN: Solution Tree Press.

DuFour, R., & Marzano, R. (2011). *Leaders of learning: How district, school and classroom leaders improve student achievement.* Bloomington, IN: Solution Tree Press.

Elmore, R. (2000). *Building a new structure for school leadership.* New York, NY: Albert Shanker Institute.

Fry, L. W., & Nisiewicz, M. S. (2013). *Maximizing the triple bottom line through spiritual leadership.* Stanford, CA: Stanford University Press.

Green, R. (2017). *Practicing the art of leadership.* (5th ed.). New York, NY: Pearson.

Greenleaf, R. (1977). *Servant leadership: A journey into the nature of legitimate power and greatness.* New York, NY: Paulist Press.

Hallinger, P., Murphy, M., Well, M., Mesa, R., & Mitman, A. (1983). Identifying the specific practices, behaviors for principals. *NASSP Bulletin, 67*(463), 83–91.

Hargreaves, A., & Boyle, A. (2015). Uplifting leadership. *Educational Leadership, 72*(5), 42–47.

Harvey, E., Cottrell, D., & Lucia, A. (2003). *The leadership secrets of Santa Claus.* Dallas, TX: Walk the Talk.

Hattie, J. (2015). High impact leadership. *Educational Leadership, 72*(5), 36–40.

Hattie, J., Masters, D., & Birch, K. (in press). *Visible learning into action: International case studies of impact.* New York, NY: Routledge.

Hersey, P., & Blanchard, K. (1982). *Management of organizational behavior: Utilizing human resources.* (4th ed.). Englewood Cliffs, NJ: Prentice Hall.

Interstate School Leaders Licensure Consortium. (2008). *ISLLC standards.* Washington, DC: Interstate School Leaders Licensure Consortium and Chief State School Officers.

Leithwood, K. (1994). Leadership for school restructuring. *Educational Administration Quarterly, 30*(4), 498–518.

Leithwood, K., & Riehl, C. (2003). *What we know about successful school leadership.* Philadelphia, PA: Laboratory for Student Success, Temple University.

Lewin, K., Lippitt, R., & White, R. (1939). Patterns of aggressive behavior in experimentally created "social climates." *Journal of Science Psychology, 10,* 271–299.

Likert, R. (1961). *New patterns of management.* New York, NY: McGraw-Hill.

Likert, R. (1967). *The human organization: Its management and value.* New York, NY: McGraw-Hill.

Marks, H., & Printy, S. (2003). Principal leadership and school performance: An integration of transformational and instructional leadership. *Educational Administration Quarterly, 39*(3), 370–397.

Marzano, R., & Waters, T. (2009). *District leadership that works: Striking the right balance.* Bloomington, IN: Solution Tree Press.

Marzano, R., Waters, T., & McNulty, B. (2005). *School leadership that works: From research to results.* Alexandria, VA: Association for Supervision and Curriculum Development.

Maxwell, J. (1995). *Developing the leaders around you: How to help others reach their full potential*. Nashville, TN: Thomas Nelson.

McGregor, D. (1960). *The human side of enterprise*. New York, NY: McGraw-Hill.

Nanus, B. (1992). *Visionary leadership: Creating a compelling sense of direction for your organization*. San Francisco, CA: Jossey-Bass.

Northouse, P. (2012). *Introduction to leadership*. (2nd ed.). Thousand Oaks, CA: Sage.

Robinson, V., Lloyd, C., & Rowe, K. (2008). The impact of leadership on student outcomes: An analysis of the differential effects of leadership types. *Educational Administration Quarterly, 44*(5), 635–674.

Scharmer, O. (2009). *Theory U: Leading from the future as it emerges*. San Francisco, CA: Berrett-Koehler.

Sergiovanni, T. (1992). *Moral leadership: Getting to the heart of school improvement*. San Francisco, CA: Jossey-Bass.

Sergiovanni, T. (1999). *Rethinking leadership*. Glenview, IL: Skylight.

Siccone, F. (2012). *Essential skills for effective leadership*. New York, NY: Pearson.

Smith, W., & Andrews, R. (1989). *Instructional leadership: How principals make a difference*. Alexandria, VA: Association for Supervision and Curriculum Development.

Smoker, M. (2011). *Focus: Elevating the essentials to radically improve student learning*. Alexandria, VA: Association for Supervision and Curriculum Development.

Spears, L. (1995). *Reflections on leadership: How Robert K. Greenleaf's servant leadership influenced today's top management thinkers*. New York, NY: Wiley Press.

Spillane, J., & Sherer, J. Z. (2004). A distributed perspective on school leadership: Leadership practice as stretched over people and place. The Distributive Leadership Study: Northwestern University.

Stogdill, R. (1948). Personal factors associated with leadership: A survey of the literature. *Journal of Psychology, 25*, 35–71.

Stogdill, R. (1974). *Handbook of leadership*. New York, NY: Free Press.

Stogdill, R., & Coons, A. (1957). *Leader behavior: Its description and measurement*. Columbus, OH: Ohio State University.

Warwick, R. (2015). *The challenge for school leaders: A new way of thinking about leadership*. Lanham, MD: Rowman & Littlefield.

CHAPTER FIVE

Linking Theories and Standards to *The Leadership Framework*

Leadership is practiced not so much in words than in attitude and actions.

—Harold S. Geneen

Objectives

At the conclusion of this chapter you will be able to:

1. Apply concepts of *The Leadership Framework* as they relate to practices (PSEL 1, 2, 3, 4, 5, 6, 7, 8, 9, 10; NELP 1, 2, 3, 4, 5, 6, 7, 8).
2. Apply concepts of the PSEL (2015) as they relate to *The Leadership Framework* and effective leadership theory practices (PSEL 1, 2, 3, 4, 5, 6, 7, 8, 9, 10; NELP 1, 2, 3, 4, 5, 6, 7, 8).
3. Synthesize an educational platform that assimilates the PSEL (2015), *The Leadership Framework*, and leadership theories (PSEL 1, 2, 3, 4, 5, 6, 7, 8, 9, 10; NELP 1, 2, 3, 4, 5, 6, 7, 8).

The Need for a Framework

Bolden, Gosling, Marturano, and Dennison (2003) conducted a research study, titled A *Review of Leadership Theory and Competency Frameworks*, through the University of Exeter in the United Kingdom. In the study, the authors concluded that British organizations concerned about effective leadership, both in the private and public sectors, needed to do two things. First, they needed to identify and define the qualities of effective leaders. Second, they needed to create leadership development frameworks or processes to ensure continuing effective leadership.

Examples of leadership models and competency frameworks in British companies examined in that 2003 study were the Lufthansa Leadership Compass, the Astra Zeneca Leadership Capabilities, Federal Express Leadership Qualities, Senior Civil Service Competency Framework, Shell Oil, and the National College for School Leadership-Hay McBer Model. One example is the Shell Oil Leadership Developmental Model, which included four attributes: authenticity (professionalism and resilience), growth (value), collaboration (strong partnerships), and performance (business outcomes, invest in people and teams).

The National College for School Leadership in the United Kingdom created a *leadership development framework* (Bolden et al., 2003), which had 10 propositions for school leadership. School leaders must:

1. Be purposeful, inclusive, and value driven
2. Embrace the distinctive and inclusive context of the school
3. Promote an active view of learning
4. Be instructionally focused
5. Be a function that is distributed throughout the school community
6. Build capacity by developing the school as a learning community
7. Be future oriented and strategically driven
8. Be developed through experiential and innovative technologies
9. Be served by a support and policy context that is coherent and implementation driven
10. Be supported by a National College that leads the discourse around leadership for learning (p. 27)

The National College for Teaching and Leadership (2015) in the United Kingdom ensures the National Professional Qualification for Headship. This process outlines how to develop the skills, knowledge, and confidence that potential leaders need to become highly effective head teachers. Three essential modules are required: leading and improving teaching, leading an effective school, and successful headship. Further study is required through completion of two additional modules of choice in areas such as closing the gap, curriculum development, freedoms and constraints, relationships and reputation, or leading staff and effective teams. A final assessment is required.

This British study is a great example of the need to articulate the qualities of leadership and develop frameworks and systems to train future leaders in these qualities in both public and private business sectors. In educational leadership, this needs to be done as well.

The purpose of this chapter is to demonstrate the connections between the PSEL (2015), *The Leadership Framework*, and the theories of educational leadership. In this chapter, the PSEL (2015) will be presented and then linked with the four domains, 18 components, and 90 elements of *The Leadership Framework*. Appropriate theories of leadership will be matched to the PSEL (2015) and to *The Leadership Framework*.

The purpose of *The Leadership Framework* is to provide a domain format useful for facilitating supervision and evaluation of school leaders that leads to deeper conversations and professional growth opportunities. *The Leadership Framework* uses clear and specific rubrics to identify and define effective school leadership knowledge, skills, dispositions, and practices.

Connecting Standards, Theories, and *The Leadership Framework*

The Interstate School Leaders Licensure Consortium (ISLLC) standards were first developed in 1996 by the Council of Chief State School Officers (CCSSO), a national organization of public school officials from all 50 states. The CCSSO developed a set of common standards that provided an outline of what effective school leaders (practicing and aspiring) should know (content knowledge) and be able to do (practices and skills) and what dispositions they should possess (attitudes).

The significance of the formation of the ISLLC standards was that this was the first major attempt to provide an outline of the principles of effective leadership. Each of the six standards contributed to an outline of the foundational principles of effective educational leadership that promoted the success of all students. In 2008, the ISLLC standards were revised, and indicators became functions.

Revised again in 2015, the ISLLC standards were renamed the PSEL (Professional Standards for Educational Leaders), and changes resulted in an increase from 6 to 10 standards. The focus is on the importance of each student learning and the foundational principles of leadership. The core standards are standard 4 (curriculum, instruction, and assessment) and standard 5 (community of care and support for students). These two standards remind effective educational leaders that their main focus is on developing a rigorous system of learning but also an inclusive, caring, and supportive community that promotes student academic success and the well-being of each student.

This is a shift from the previous ISLLC standards in that leaders are expected to develop a whole child emphasis of academic and social-emotional learning. The driver standards include mission, vision, and core values (standard 1); ethics and professional norms (standard 2); equity and cultural responsiveness (standard 3); and school improvement (standard 10). The driver standards provide the foundation and core values for the academic success and well-being of students.

The supports standards include standard 6 (professional capacity of school personnel), standard 7 (professional community for teachers and staff), standard 8 (meaningful engagement of families and community), and standard 9 (operations and management). These support standards define specific direction to effective leaders to provide all that is needed to achieve student academic success and well-being in addition to helping the faculty and staff. The standards provide a shared vision of what school leaders should know and be able to do to effectively lead today's schools. Table 5.1 provides an overview of the changes within the ISLLC standards.

Table 5.1. Correlation of ISLLC Standards (2008) with Learning Forward (2011), PSEL (2015), and NELP Standards (2018)

ISLLC Standards (2008)	Learning Forward Standards for Professional Learning (2011)	PSEL (2015)	NELP Standards (2018)
Standard 1: Vision	Learning communities: continuous improvement, collective responsibility, alignment and accountability Data: analyze student, educator, and system data; assess progress; evaluate professional learning	Standard 1: Mission, vision, and core values Standard 10: School improvement	Standard 1: Mission, vision, and improvement

ISLLC Standards (2008)	Learning Forward Standards for Professional Learning (2011)	PSEL (2015)	NELP Standards (2018)
Standard 2: School culture and instructional program	Learning designs: apply learning theories, research, and models; select learning designs; promote active engagement Outcomes: meet performance standards, address learning outcomes, build coherence	Standard 4: Curriculum, instruction, and assessment Standard 5: Community of care and support for students Standard 6: Professional capacity of school personnel Standard 7: Professional community for teachers and staff	Standard 4: Learning and instruction Standard 5: Community and external leadership Standard 7: Building professional capacity
Standard 3: Operations, management, and resources	Resources: prioritize human, fiscal, material, technology, and time resources; monitor resources; coordinate resources	Standard 5: Community of care and support for students Standard 6: Professional capacity of school personnel Standard 9: Operations and management	Standard 5: Community and external leadership Standard 6: Operations and management Standard 7: Building professional capacity
Standard 4: Collaboration with families/ community	Leadership: develop capacity for learning and leading, advocate for professional learning, and create support systems and structures	Standard 8: Meaningful engagement of families and community	Standard 5: Community and external leadership
Standard 5: Acts with integrity and fairness and ethically	Leadership: develop capacity for learning and leading, advocate for professional learning, and create support systems and structures	Standard 2: Ethics and professional norms Standard 3: Equity and cultural responsiveness	Standard 2: Ethics and professional norms Standard 3: Equity, inclusiveness, and cultural responsiveness
Standard 6: Political, social, legal, and cultural contexts	Implementation: apply change research, sustain implementation, provide constructive feedback	Standard 3: Equity and cultural responsiveness Standard 8: Meaningful engagement of families and community	Standard 3: Equity, inclusiveness, and cultural responsiveness Standard 5: Community and external leadership Standard 8: internships

This next segment provides a comprehensive look at the alignment between the PSEL (2015), *The Leadership Framework*, and leadership theories. In addition, each component and element directly align to the PSEL to demonstrate they are evidence based. Table 5.2 provides an overview of the crosswalk that demonstrates the connections between PSEL, *The Leadership Framework*, and leadership theories followed by the narrative explanation for each connection within the crosswalk.

Table 5.2. Connecting the PSEL (2015) to *The Leadership Framework* and Theories of Leadership

PSEL (2015)	The Leadership Framework	Theories of Leadership
1. Mission, vision, and core values	Domain 1a, b, c	Distributed leadership Symbolic and cultural leadership
2. Ethics and professional norms	Domain 1d, e	Transformational leadership Uplifting leadership
3. Equity and cultural responsiveness	Domain 1d, e Domain 3a, b Domain 4e	Successful/effective leadership Situational instructional leadership Moral leadership
4. Curriculum, instruction, and assessment	Domain 3a, b, c, d	Instructional leadership High impact instructional leadership
5. Community of care and support for students	Domain 1b, d, e	Servant leadership Distributed leadership
6. Professional capacity of school personnel	Domain 1a, b, c, d, e Domain 2a, b, c, d Domain 3a, b, c, d Domain 4a, b, c, d, e	Uplifting leadership High impact instructional leadership
7. Professional community for teachers and staff	Domain 1a, b, c, e Domain 2a, b, c, d	Transformational leadership Distributed leadership Servant leadership Moral leadership Uplifting leadership
8. Meaningful engagement of families and community	Domain 1a, c Domain 4d	Servant leadership Distributed leadership Situational leadership
9. Operations and management	Domain 4a, b, c, d, e	Situational awareness Distributed leadership Total quality management leadership
10. School improvement	Domain 1a, b, c, d, e Domain 2a, b, c, d Domain 3a, b, c, d Domain 4a, b, c, d, e	Professional learning communities and collaboration Distributed leadership

PSEL Standard 1: Mission, Vision, and Core Values

"Effective educational leaders develop, articulate, advocate, and enact a shared mission, vision, and core values of high quality education and academic success and well-being of each student."

The following seven elements elaborate on the work necessary to meet this standard. Effective leaders (a) Develop an educational mission for the school to promote the academic success and well-being of each student; (b) In collaboration with members of the school and community and using relevant data, develop and promote a vision for the school on the successful learning and development of each child and on instructional and organizational practices that promote such success; (c) articulate, advocate, and cultivate core values that define the school's culture and stress the imperative of child-centered education, high expectations and student support, equity, inclusiveness, social justice, openness, caring, trust, and continuous improvement; (d) strategically develop, implement, and evaluate actions to achieve the vision of the school; (e) review the school's mission and vision and adjust them to changing expectations and opportunities for the school and changing needs and situations of students; (f) develop shared understanding of and commitment to mission, vision, and core values within the school and the community; and (g) model and pursue the school's mission, vision, and core values in all aspects of school leadership.

The Leadership Framework Domain 1: Leadership Competencies 1a, 1b, and 1c

The Leadership Framework 1a establishes a solid foundation of leadership competencies. Effective leaders help develop and uphold the mission, vision, values, and goals of the school that lead to quality teaching and learning. These leaders also identify benchmarks, expectations, and feedback measures to ensure accountability. All of this is done by building quality relationships with all stakeholders. Effective leaders are accessible, approachable, and engaged in all aspects of the school.

Effective school leaders live the school and/or district's vision, mission, goals, and values by what they say and more so through their actions. Leaders remind all educators where they want to be, who they are, and what is most important for their community. Educators need this reminder because they are often bogged down with the busyness of everyday schooling and forget the core priorities of their profession.

The Leadership Framework 1b promotes building shared leadership through collaboration with others, advocating for staff and students, delegating, and building professional growth of all staff and leadership team members. An effective leader needs to work to build consensus with all stakeholders. Innovative thinking and risk taking of all stakeholders is also encouraged.

The *Leadership Framework* 1c focuses on effective communication that articulates, recognizes, facilitates, promotes, considers, and elicits all members of the community sharing the mission, vision, and core values of the school. An effective leader articulates, advocates, cultivates, and reviews the school's mission, vision, and core values and adjusts them to the changing needs of the school. Leaders develop a shared understanding of the mission, vision, and core values and model these in all aspects of leadership.

Leadership Theory

In order to accomplish all this, effective leaders must practice *distributed leadership* (Elmore, 2000; Spillane & Scherer, 2004). By involving all stakeholders, effective school leaders are encouraging buy-in or common ownership. The work of leadership competencies includes establishing a solid foundation and building shared leadership.

Another leadership theory that addresses the mission, vision, and core values is what Sergiovanni (1999) identifies as *symbolic and cultural leadership*. Effective school leaders practice *symbolic leadership* when they point educators to improvement by painting a canvas of what the school could become. This is the vision of the school community. Added to this is *cultural leadership* in which effective school leaders constantly proclaim the purpose of the school and their identity as a special people who make a difference with the students they serve. A key question always to ask is, "How will this help our students excel as learners?" This is the true mission of the school community.

PSEL Standard 2: Ethics and Professional Norms

"Effective educational leaders act ethically and according to professional norms to promote each student's academic success and well-being."

The following six elements elaborate on the work necessary to meet this standard. Effective leaders (a) act ethically and professionally in personal conduct, relationships with others, decision-making, stewardship of the school's resources, and all aspects of school leadership; (b) act accordingly to and promote the professional norms of integrity, fairness, transparency, trust, collaboration, perseverance, learning, and continuous improvement; (c) place children at the center of education and accept responsibility for each teacher's academic success and well-being; (d) safeguard and promote the values of democracy, individual freedom and responsibility, equity, social justice, community, and diversity; (e) lead with interpersonal and communication skill, social-emotional insight, and understanding of all students' and staff members' backgrounds and cultures; and (f) provide moral direction for the school and promote ethical and professional behavior among faculty and staff.

The Leadership Framework Domain 1: Leadership Competencies 1d and 1e

Ethics and professional norms are addressed in Domain 1d. School leaders are expected to adhere to a moral compass in component 1d by modeling integrity, fairness, honesty, and respect and maintaining professional dispositions. Starratt (1994) asserted a model of ethics, including the ethic of care, the ethic of justice, and the ethic of critique. Effective school leaders need to address the various questions that arise from each of these types of ethics.

The ethic of care is building relationships with others that included modeling (demonstrate that you care), dialogue (open ended and sincere), practice (listening fully), and confirmation (calling forth the best self of the other). The ethic of justice seeks fairness and equity and invites school leaders to question themselves. The ethic of critique invites school leaders to question and dialogue with others to challenge the status quo. Two key questions are, Who benefits from this? Whose voice has not been heard?

According to Cordeiro and Cunningham (2013), every professional organization has a code of ethics or professional norms that everyone is expected to practice. For school leaders, the norms might be honesty, integrity, due process, civil and human rights, and the well-being of every student. A code of ethics should be part of the philosophy and practice of every effective school leader.

Ethics and professional norms are also addressed in 1e—promoting a positive school culture. Effective educational leaders establish an environment of trust, tolerance, respect, and rapport that advocates for equity, fairness, and diversity. Sustaining a safe and educationally sound climate, responding to the needs of stakeholders, demonstrating cultural responsiveness, and encouraging inquiry and reflection are also other focuses of these effective educational leaders.

Leadership Theory

Adhering to ethics and professional norms are examples of *transformational leadership* (Burns, 1978) in which the school leader and educators are bound together by sharing common beliefs, values, and norms. By practicing these common ideals, the participants are transformed. Hargreaves and Boyle (2015) refer to this as *uplifting leadership* because, through this experience of ethics and professional norms, the spirits, hopes, and the performances of people are raised.

PSEL Standard 3: Equity and Cultural Responsiveness

"Effective educational leaders strive for equity of educational opportunity and culturally responsive practices to promote each student's academic success and well-being."

The following eight elements elaborate on the work necessary to meet this standard. Effective leaders (a) ensure that each student is treated fairly and respectfully and with an understanding of each student's culture and context; (b) recognize, respect, and employ each student's strengths, diversity, and culture as assets for teaching and learning; (c) ensure that each student has equitable access to effective teachers, learning opportunities, academic and social support, and other resources necessary for success; (d) develop student policies and address student misconduct in a positive, fair, and unbiased manner; (e) confront and alter institutional biases of student marginalization, deficit-based schooling, and low expectations associated with race, class, culture and language, gender and sexual orientation, and disability or special status; (f) promote the preparation of students to live productively in and contribute to the diverse cultural contexts of a global society; (g) act with cultural competence and responsiveness in their interactions, decision-making, and practice; and (h) address matters of equity and cultural responsiveness in all aspects of leadership.

The Leadership Framework Domain 1: Leadership Competencies 1d and 1e; Domain 3: Instructional Practices 3a and 3b; and Domain 4: Management Competencies 4e

In *The Leadership Framework* 1d, effective schools leaders are charged to adhere to a moral compass that includes modeling integrity, fairness, honesty, and respect. Further, these leaders are asked to demonstrate the application of ethics and justice by understanding the cultural context of the community.

The Leadership Framework 1e invites effective school leaders to promote school culture in an environment where there is trust, tolerance, respect, rapport, equity, fairness, and diversity. These components demonstrate cultural responsiveness and lead to an environment where all stakeholders feel safe and in a proper educationally sound climate.

In *The Leadership Framework* 3a, effective school leaders are expected to demand equity and accessibility of curriculum and resources for all students and educators. *The Leadership Framework* 3b adds to this by describing these leaders as advocates for instruction that supports the needs of all learners. *The Leadership Framework* 4e asserts that it is the management responsibility of leaders to oversee these systems and processes of equity and cultural responsiveness.

Equity and cultural responsiveness deal with the issue of diversity. Schools across the country are struggling to understand and to respond to the growing diversity within their communities. School leaders must lead the way in responding in an appropriate manner. The University of Tennessee Libraries Diversity Committee (2015) defined diversity this way:

> Diversity is a commitment to recognizing and appreciating the variety of characteristics that make individuals unique in an atmosphere that promotes and celebrates individual and collective achievement. Examples of these characteristics are: age; cognitive style; culture; disability (mental, learning, physical); economic background; education; ethnicity; gender identity; geographic background; language(s) spoken; marital/partnered status; physical appearance; political affiliation; race; religious beliefs; sexual orientation.

This is a powerful statement of what diversity could be that ensures equity and cultural responsiveness. Effective school leaders must lead the charge for educators to address and respond to the needs of diverse populations in their school communities.

Leadership Theory

Leithwood and Riehl (2003) assert that school leaders need to develop people within the organization. They called this *successful or effective leadership*. In terms of equity and cultural responsiveness, this means providing an appropriate model. Effective school leaders should be the example to all members of the school community by modeling the core value of diversity. It is not just tolerating differences but ensuring, fostering, advocating, attacking, promoting, and monitoring diversity.

Hersey and Blanchard (1982) described *situational leadership* in which effective leaders adjust their leadership style and behavior to the experience and expertise of the followers. In doing so, these effective leaders meet the demands of this standard of equity and cultural responsiveness. *Moral leadership* (Sergovanni, 1992) is a theory that also meets this standard in that effective leaders do the right thing for their students, teachers, and parents when they balance the head, the heart, and the hand.

PSEL Standard 4: Curriculum, Instruction, and Assessment

"Effective educational leaders develop and support intellectually rigorous and coherent systems of curriculum, instruction, and assessment to promote each student's academic success and well-being."

The following seven elements elaborate on the work necessary to meet this standard. Effective leaders (a) implement coherent systems of curriculum, instruction, and assessment that promote the mission, vision, and core values of the school; embody high expectations for student learning; align with academic standards; and are culturally responsive; (b) align and focus systems of curriculum, instruction, and assessment within and across grade levels to promote student academic success; love of learning; the identities and habits of learners; and healthy sense of self; (c) promote instructional practice that is consistent with knowledge of child learning and development, effective pedagogy, and the needs of each student; (d) ensure instructional practice that is intellectually challenging, authentic to student experiences, recognizes student strengths, and is differentiated and personalized; (e) promote the effective use of technology in the service of teaching and learning; (f) employ valid assessments that are consistent with knowledge of child learning and development and technical standards of measurement; and (g) use assessment data appropriately and within technical limitations to monitor student progress and improve instruction.

The Leadership Framework Domain 3: Instructional Practices 3a, 3b, 3c, and 3d

The Leadership Framework 3a focuses on effective school leaders who champion and support curriculum development. This involves developing, implementing, and revising curriculum based on indicators of student success and needs. The Common Core State Standards (CCSSO, 2019) are a foundation in curriculum development that provide for educators newer, fewer, higher, and clearer standards to ensure college and career readiness for all students.

The Leadership Framework 3b asserts that effective school leaders are advocates for instruction that supports the needs of all learners. This means that school leaders must encourage differentiated instruction. Not all students are the same. Educators must adjust their instructional strategies to the needs of individual students and invite students to take ownership of their own learning pathways. Instruction, therefore, needs to be engaging, rigorous, and relevant to the needs of students. Further, students and educators must be given high expectations and be challenged. Effective leaders do not allow people to remain at the status quo level. Instead they model, mentor, encourage, support, and provide opportunities to move people to the next level.

The Leadership Framework 3c suggests that effective school leaders and all educators analyze assessments. Student learning is the product of curricula and assessment programs. Effective school leaders need to engage all staff in an effort to clearly define what they want students to know and be able to do by the end of a class, unit, or semester. McTighe and Wiggins (2013) address these issues in their book *Essential Questions: Opening Doors to Student Understanding*.

The Leadership Framework 3d calls for effective school leaders to incorporate technology to enhance learning for all students and educators. In order to fulfill this challenge, educators and students must be educated in upgrades to and uses of technology. Fiscal resources and ongoing learning must be made available to students and educators through technology support staff.

Technology calls for dedicated funds, ongoing commitment, and the support of community members. Funds can come from the tax base, donations, and grants. Board members need to know and support the technology plan. Parents need to provide time, finances, and the use of their talents. School personnel need to provide peer training and share their resources. Students need to sign and agree to the usage agreement.

Marzano, Waters, and McNulty (2005) stress that second-order change can happen only when the principal's responsibilities focus on knowledge of the curriculum, instruction, and assessment; optimism; intellectual stimulation; being a change agent; monitoring and evaluating; flexibility; and ideals and beliefs. Each of these responsibilities leads to articulation of the vision of learning.

Leadership Theory

Robinson, Lloyd, and Rowe (2008) found that effective instructional leaders were focused on students, student learning, and instructional issues. This is *instructional leadership*. Hattie (2015) added to this by suggesting that effective school leaders practiced *high impact instructional leadership* when they led their schools focused on seven major mind frames. (See chapter 4 where these mind frames are discussed.)

Effective educational leaders develop and support intellectually rigorous and coherent systems of curriculum, instruction, and assessment when they can articulate the content of each of these areas but also when they are working hands on with teachers in each of these areas. Marzano et al. (2005) describe this as being directly involved and as also having extensive knowledge of these areas. This may include helping teachers design curriculum projects, create assessments, and work on instructional strategies that engage students. Identifying key student data and revising strategies of assessment are major expectations of effective leaders today. Understanding new techniques and use of technology in the classroom are also areas of concern that effective school leaders must address today.

PSEL Standard 5: Community of Care and Support for Students

"Effective educational leaders cultivate an inclusive, caring, and supportive school community that promotes the academic success and well-being of each student."

The following six elements elaborate on the work necessary to meet this standard. Effective leaders (a) build and maintain a safe, caring, and healthy school environment that meets the academic, social, emotional, and physical needs of each student; (b) create and sustain a school environment in which each student is known, accepted and valued, trusted and respected, cared for, and encouraged to be an active and responsible member of the school community; (c) provide coherent systems of academic and social supports, services, extracurricular activities, and accommodations to meet the range of learning needs of each student; (d) promote adult–student, student–peer, and school–community relationships that value and support academic learning and positive social and emotional development; (e) cultivate and reinforce student engagement in school and positive student conduct; and (f) infuse the school's learning environment with the cultures and languages of the school's community.

The Leadership Framework Domain 1: Leadership Competencies 1b, 1d, and 1e

The Leadership Framework 1b proposes that effective school leaders build shared leadership. One element states that leaders advocate for staff and students. As school leaders, a key responsibility is to build relationships with teachers, staff, and students. This forms a sense of community for all stakeholders. Once this community is formed, another responsibility of effective school leaders is to promote the interests of the stakeholders, especially the students, by advocating for them in the larger community of the neighborhood, the district, and the state. The focus is on caring for students not only academically but also personally.

The Leadership Framework 1d is a component that states that effective school leaders adhere to a moral compass. One element of this is that leaders model and apply an understanding of the cultural context of the community. According to Gruenert and Whitaker (2015), the building blocks of culture are climate, mission, and vision; language; humor; routines; rituals and ceremonies; norms; roles; symbols; stories; heroes; values; and beliefs and the set of understandings or meanings shared by a group of people. It is what people say, how they behave, and how things work in a school. A culture of caring empowers all to feel a sense of belonging in the school community.

An inclusive school climate means that all students, parents, teachers, and staff feel welcome in the school. Climate is that overwhelming feeling that people have about the school. Is it warm and welcoming, or is it cold and sterile? When people feel welcome, they are more committed to the school and more productive.

Tableman and Herron (2004) suggested that there are four aspects to climate. One element is a physical environment that is welcoming and conducive to learning. An example of this is that students feel safe and comfortable. Another example is that classrooms are clean and well maintained. A second element of climate is a social environment that promotes communication and interaction. This is exemplified when interaction between students, teachers, leaders, and parents is encouraged. Another example is that student groupings are diverse.

A third element of climate is an affective environment that promotes a sense of belonging and self-esteem. An example of this is when the interactions are caring, responsive, supportive, and respectful. Additionally, this is when teachers, professional staff, and students feel they are contributing to the success of the school and a sense of community develops.

A fourth element of climate is an academic environment that promotes learning and self-fulfillment. An example of this includes high expectations for all, and student progress is monitored regularly. All types of intelligence and competence are respected and supported. A further example is that teaching methods respect the different ways and modalities in which students learn.

The Leadership Framework 1e is a component that suggests that effective school leaders promote a positive school culture. Elements of this include establishing an environment of trust, tolerance, respect, and rapport that supports equity, fairness, and diversity. This builds a community of caring for students and adults. Culturally responsive teaching is an example of this. School leaders must also sustain a safe and educationally sound climate. Having a school safety plan exemplifies this focus on safety in light of the many recent school shootings. An ongoing school improvement plan is an indicator of having an educationally sound climate.

Leadership Theory

In order to provide this community of care for students, school leaders must be committed to *servant leadership* (Greenleaf, 1977; Spears, 1995). Leaders must also be courageous in inviting other adults in the school to serve the students not only academically but also personally. This type of service is also based in *transformational leadership* (Burns, 1978) in which school leaders envision the changes that can happen in students when the adults care for the students.

A further leadership theory that provides this caring for students is *distributed leadership* (Elmore, 2000; Spillane & Scherer, 2004). School leaders need to remind all adult stakeholders in the school that everyone is important in working together to create and sustain this community of care for students.

PSEL Standard 6: Professional Capacity of School Personnel

"Effective educational leaders develop the professional capacity and practice of school personnel to promote each student's academic success and well-being."

The following nine elements elaborate on the work necessary to meet this standard. Effective leaders (a) recruit, hire, support, develop, and retain effective and caring teachers and other professional staff and form them into an educationally effective faculty; (b) plan for and manage staff turnover and succession, providing opportunities for effective induction and mentoring of new personnel; (c) develop teachers' and staff members' professional knowledge, skills, and practice through differentiated opportunities for learning and growth, guided by understanding of professional and adult learning and development; (d) foster continuous improvement of individual and collective instructional capacity to achieve outcomes envisioned for each student; (e) deliver actionable feedback about instruction and other professional practice through valid research-anchored systems of supervision and evaluation to support the development of teachers' and staff members' knowledge, skills, and practice; (f) empower and motivate teachers and staff to the highest levels of professional practice and to continuous learning and improvement; (g) develop the capacity, opportunities, and support for teacher leadership and leadership from other members of the school community; (h) promote the personal and professional health, well-being, and work–life balance of faculty and staff; and (i) tend to their own learning and effectiveness through reflection, study, and improvement, maintaining a healthy work–life balance.

The Leadership Framework Domain 1a, 1b, 1c, 1d, and 1e; Domain 2: Professional Learning and Growth Practices 2a, 2b, 2c, and 2d; Domain 3: Instructional Practices 3a, 3b, 3c, and 3d; and Domain 4: Management Competencies 4a, 4b, 4c, 4d, and 4e

All of the components and elements in Domain 1: Leadership Competencies promote a professional culture for teachers and staff. *The Leadership Framework* 1a explains that effective school leaders develop and uphold the mission, vision, values, and goals of the school. These leaders also build caring and effective relationships with all stakeholders.

In *The Leadership Framework* 1b, effective school leaders are described as people who build shared leadership and work collaboratively with all stakeholders. *The Leadership Framework* 1c adds to this by inviting leaders to initiate effective communication in which programs, progress, and needs are articulated and the accomplishments of students and staff are communicated and celebrated.

The Leadership Framework 1d asserts that effective school leaders adhere to a moral compass. This means maintaining professional dispositions of all educators and encouraging all to higher levels of commitment, performance, and motivation. Element 1d adds by encouraging leaders to promote a positive school culture.

The Leadership Framework Domain 2: Professional Learning and Growth Practices 2a, 2b, 2c, and 2d add further dimensions to what promoting a professional culture for teachers and staff might become. Effective school leaders actively participate in professional learning, provide mentoring and coaching opportunities, foster and facilitate continual improvement, promote professional learning and growth, and support school personnel.

A professional culture for teachers and staff is also developed by addressing the *Leadership Framework* Domain 3: Instructional Practices 3a, 3b, 3c, and 3d. Effective school leaders must champion and support curriculum development, advocate for instruction that supports the needs of all learners, analyze assessments, and incorporate technology to enhance learning.

In focusing on the management competencies of *The Leadership Framework*, Domains 4a, 4b, 4c, 4d, and 4e, effective school leaders should adhere to personnel requirements, report accurately and timely, uphold rules and regulations, practice and refine resourcefulness, and manage effectively. The components and elements of Domain 4 also add to building a professional culture for teachers and staff.

Leadership Theory

Hargreaves and Boyle (2015) called this focus on instruction *uplifting leadership*, in which the effective leader raised the spirits and the performances of all. In *high impact instructional leadership*, Hattie (2015) asserted that effective school leaders set challenging targets for themselves, teachers, and professional staff to maximize student outcomes.

In PSEL Standard 6, Professional Capacity of School Personnel, the focus is the investments school districts must make in the professional learning of all faculty and staff. This becomes more significant with the decline of teacher and principal recruitment and retention rates over the past decades. Teachers and principals are the foundational stones of our schools. In order to reverse these negative rates of recruitment and retention, they must be supported. The elements of PSEL Standard 6 and Standard 7 are concrete steps as how to reverse this trend of recruitment and retention.

In PSEL Standard 7, the Professional Community for Teachers and Staff, the focus is on forming a professional community where work conditions, collective responsibility, mutual accountability, and caring and trusting working relationships lead to a collaborative examination of practice, collegial feedback, and collective learning. These two PSEL standards add depth to the previous ISLLC standards.

PSEL Standard 7: Professional Community for Teachers and Staff

"Effective educational leaders foster a professional community of teachers and other professional staff to promote each student's academic success and well-being."

The following eight elements elaborate on the work necessary to meet this standard. Effective leaders (a) develop workplace conditions for teachers and other professional staff that promote effective professional development, practice, and student learning; (b) empower and entrust teachers and staff with collective responsibility for meeting the academic, social, emotional, and physical needs of each student, pursuant to the mission, vision, and core values of the school; (c) establish and sustain a professional culture of engagement and commitment to shared vision, goals, and objectives pertaining to the education of the whole child, high expectations of professional work, ethical and equitable practice, trust and open communication, collaboration, collective efficacy, and continuous individual and organizational learning and improvement; (d) promote mutual accountability among teachers and other professional staff for each student's success and the effectiveness of the school as a whole; (e) develop and support open, productive, caring, and trusting working relationships among leaders, faculty, and staff to promote professional capacity and the improvement of practice; (f) design and implement job-imbedded and other opportunities for professional learning collaboratively with faculty and staff; (g) provide opportunities for collaborative examination of practice, collegial feedback, and collective learning; and (h) encourage faculty-initiated improvement of programs and practices.

The Leadership Framework Domain 1: Leadership Competencies 1a, 1b, 1c, and 1e; Domain 2: Professional Learning and Growth Practices 2a, 2b, 2c, and 2d

In the *Leadership Framework*, Leadership Competencies 1a asserts that effective leaders must establish a foundation of the mission, vision, core values, and goals of the school in order to foster a professional community for teachers and staff. Everyone in the school community must be in agreement with who they are, what they value, and where they are going. If not, they most likely will go in different directions. At the beginning of each school year, the school community must reaffirm their mission, vision, core values, and goals, and throughout the year these foundational statements must be used as a measuring tool to assess how they are doing on reaching student academic success and well-being.

Element 1b states that effective leaders must foster professional community and shared leadership through working collaboratively, promoting of teacher leaders, delegating tasks, building consensus, and supporting innovative thinking. Element 1c affirms that effective leaders can foster community through initiating effective communication that uses a variety of means, provides progress and needs, recognizes and celebrates accomplishments of all, facilitates professional dialogue, and considers the opinions of all in decision-making.

Element 1e promotes a positive school culture as a way of fostering a professional community of all. This includes establishing an environment of trust, tolerance, respect, and rapport, advocating equity, fairness, and diversity; sustaining a safe climate; responding to needs to all stakeholders; and encouraging inquiry and reflection.

Fullan and Hargreaves (1996) and Deal and Kennedy (1999) added to the sense of professional culture for teachers and staff by introducing six types of culture that can exist within schools: collaborative, comfortable–collaborative, contrived–congenial, balkanized, fragmented, and toxic. Collaborative means that everyone works together for the good of all. This experience of collaborative culture is detailed in the eight elements of PSEL Standard 7. This standard invites teachers and staff to form a professional community where there is collective responsibility; a professional culture of engagement and commitment to shared vision, goals, and objectives; and mutual accountability among teachers and staff for student academic success and well-being.

Comfortable–collaborative culture suggests that people feel comfortable about working together to establish common goals. Contrived–congenial culture is experienced when people are nice while working together but do not go further with each other to work toward school goals and the good of all.

Balkanized culture happens when stakeholders form groups and work against each other. A fragmented culture is one in which there are many groups working in isolation. A toxic culture is an unhealthy environment where there are many negative identifiers, such as gossip and back-biting occurring. No one is working together for the good of all. Balkanized, fragmented, and toxic cultures are not good for the students. Effective school leaders must work to change these negative cultures if students are to benefit from these teachers and staff.

The Leadership Framework, Domain 2: Professional Learning and Growth Practices 2a, 2b, 2c, and 2d also help educational leaders foster professional community for teachers and staff. Effective leaders demonstrate their competence as leaders by incorporating new ideas in the district, participating in professional learning, providing mentoring and coaching opportunities, modeling accountability and responsibility, and differentiating interactions with boards and organizations. Continual improvement is facilitated by identifying areas of discourse, target areas, strategies of growth, monitoring progress of instruction, and evaluating programs and processes on a regular basis.

These effective leaders also promote professional learning and growth through ensuring commitment; providing opportunities for professional learning; using the gifts and talents of district staff to provide peer training; aligning personal and district goals; encouraging collaborative, ongoing work; and modeling lifelong learning. Finally, effective leaders support school personnel by understanding various instructional strategies, providing follow-through, protecting instructional time, and fostering a climate that supports high expectations and providing resources, time, roles, and structure imperative to promote each student's academic success and well-being.

Leadership Theory

Five leadership theories form the basis of fostering a professional community for teachers and staff. *Transformational leadership* (Burns, 1978) suggests that inspiring school leaders motivate teachers and staff to go beyond their own personal interests to build open, productive, caring, and trusting relationships. Effective school leaders practice *distributed leadership* (Elmore, 2000; Spillane & Scherer, 2004) in which a professional community is formed and in which teachers, staff, and leaders take collective responsibility and mutual accountability for student's academic success and well-being.

Servant leadership (Greenleaf, 1977; Spears, 1995) is the guiding principle of school leaders who seek to improve working conditions for teachers and staff. Effective school leaders who seek to meet the academic, social, emotional, and physical needs of each student exemplify the *moral leadership* of Sergiovanni (1992), who articulated the balancing of the head, heart, and hand of school leaders. *Uplifting leadership* (Hargreaves & Boyle, 2015) addresses leaders who raise spirits, hopes, and performances of all. This happens when effective leaders promote a professional culture of collaboration, engagement, and commitment to shared goals, vision, and objectives for the academic success and well-being of each student.

PSEL Standard 8: Meaningful Engagement of Families and Community

"Effective educational leaders engage families and the community in meaningful, reciprocal, and mutually beneficial ways to promote each student's success and well-being."

The following 10 elements elaborate on the work necessary to meet this standard. Effective leaders (a) are approachable, accessible, and welcoming to families and members of the community; (b) create and sustain positive, collaborative, and productive relationships with families and the community for the benefit of the students; (c) engage in regular and open two-way communication with families and the community about the school, students, needs, problems, and accomplishments; (d) maintain a presence in the community to understand its strengths and needs, develop productive relationships, and engage its resources for the school; (e) create means for the school community to partner with families to support student learning in and out of school; (f) understand, value, and employ the community's cultural, social, intellectual, and political resources to promote student learning and school improvement; (g) develop and provide the school as a resource for families and the community; (h) advocate for the school and the district and for the importance of education and student needs and priorities to families and the community; (i) advocate publicly for the needs and priorities of students, families, and the community; and (j) build and sustain productive partnerships with public and private sectors to promote school improvement and student learning.

The Leadership Framework Domain 1: Leadership Competencies 1a and 1c; and Domain 4 Management Competencies 4d

In The *Leadership Framework* Domain 1: Leadership Competencies, 1a asserts that effective educational leaders build caring, effective relationships with stakeholders. In PSEL Standard 8a, effective educational leaders are to be approachable, accessible, and welcoming to these families and communities. In addition, there must be two-way communication between schools, families, and communities. This is an area of concern for school leaders. Sometimes, it is difficult to connect with families and communities due to language and educational background barriers. There are many families that do not speak English, and schools do not have the resources to provide translators.

Lower income and new immigrant families may value education in a different way. Other families may have limited time to connect with the school community due to (multiple) jobs and other responsibilities. Residents of the community, regardless of age, who do not have children in school may also present a problem of lack of communication for local school leaders. And then there are those families that might be overinvolved in the school. This presents another challenge to effective school leaders.

In *The Leadership Framework* Domain 1: Leadership Competencies, 1c says that leaders also need to model and apply an understanding of the cultural context of the community. In PSEL Standard 8f, effective leaders are encouraged to value and employ the community's cultural, social, intellectual, and political resources. This is the hard work of leaders in getting to know their neighbors.

According to Cordeiro and Cunningham (2013), various community entities influence teachers, staff, school leaders, students, and families. These organizations include the medical community (local hospitals, nursing homes, and health care facilities); the media; social service agencies; business and industry; social and ethnic organizations; religious organizations; higher education institutions; nonprofit agencies; fire and police departments; local political groups; youth organizations, such as the park district, YMCA, or Boys and Girls Clubs; and the virtual community via television, Internet, and social media.

In *The Leadership Framework* Domain 4: Management Competencies, 4d challenges effective leaders to establish partnerships, investigate creative funding opportunities, and use outside resources. Partnerships (Cordeiro & Monroe-Kolek, 1996) can develop between schools and these organizations when leadership, trust, stability, readiness, and a common agenda exist. Collaboration occurs when communication between school and these organizations is positive. Aligning and pooling of resources can benefit everyone.

When the school works with these various organizations, a complementary relationship can fill the gaps in services. An example of this is when school districts share their libraries and gym facilities with local communities. A duplication of buildings is reduced, and everyone benefits from the shared resources.

Leadership Theory

Three leadership theories are the basis of meaningful engagement of families and community. *Servant leadership* (Greenleaf, 1977; Spears, 1995) is the basis for each of these organizations who seek to serve the greater needs of their communities. Second, the involvement of so many organizations in the life of students and their families is *distributed leadership* (Elmore, 2000; Spillane & Scherer, 2004) in action.

The third theory is *situational leadership* (Hersey & Blanchard, 1982) because each organization responds to the needs of the school, depending on the situation. Each organization does its part to build up the community. An effective school leader needs to know his or her communities and what resources are available.

PSEL Standard 9: Operations and Management

"Effective educational leaders manage school operations and resources to promote each student's academic success and well-being."

The following 12 elements elaborate on the work necessary to meet this standard. Effective leaders (a) institute, manage, and monitor operations and administrative systems that promote the mission and vision of the school; (b) strategically manage staff resources, assigning and scheduling teachers and staff to roles and responsibilities that optimize their professional capacity to address each student's learning needs; (c) seek, acquire, and manage fiscal, physical, and other resources to support curriculum, instruction, and assessment; student learning community; professional capacity and community; and family and community engagement; (d) are responsible, ethical, and accountable stewards of the school's monetary and nonmonetary resources, engaging in effective budgeting and accounting practices; (e) protect teachers' and other staff members' work and learning from disruption; (f) employ technology to improve the quality and efficiency of operations and management; (g) develop and maintain data and communication systems to deliver actionable information for classroom and school improvement; (h) know, comply with, and help the school community understand local, state, and federal laws, rights, policies, and regulations so as to promote student success; (i) develop and manage relationships with feeder and connecting schools for enrollment management and curricular and instructional articulation; (j) develop and manage productive relationships with the central office and the school board; (k) develop and administer systems for fair and equitable management of conflict among students, faculty, and staff; leaders; families; and community; and (l) manage governance processes and internal and external politics toward achieving the school's mission and vision.

The Leadership Framework Domain 4: Management Competencies 4a, 4b, 4c, 4d, and 4e

The Leadership Framework Domain 4 addresses management competencies. The components specified are adhering to personnel requirements, reporting accurately and timely, upholding rules and regulations, practicing and refining resourcefulness, and managing effectively. Warwick (2015) identified these operations and management procedures as the network of systems. These include the school organizational structure (the building leadership team), the communication system, the curriculum system, the instructional system, the assessment system, and the professional behaviors and values.

Leithwood and Riehl (2003) called these operations and management activities as developing the organization when school leaders attend to all aspects of the school as an organization and a community of learners. Effective leaders monitor and make adjustments as they oversee that tasks are performed and the use of time and space, the acquisition of equipment and supplies, and operating procedures are followed. The leaders are also concerned that the environment is safe and healthy to maximize teaching and learning opportunities.

Examples of managing the school effectively might include the following: creating schedules, assigning staff and personnel, participating in the school budget plan, supervising performance appraisal of instructional and noninstructional staff, and designing a school safety and security plan. Daily walkthroughs of the school by school leaders with the maintenance staff ensure that the facilities are well maintained and repaired as needed.

Addressing faculty, staff, and student behavior problems is also a part of the management of the discipline system of the school. Communication is also an important system that effective school leaders must manage. School leaders make sure that all stakeholders know what is going on in the school through such venues as newsletters, e-mails, bulletins, social media, websites (district, school, and classroom), text messages, phone calls, and meetings with individuals and groups.

Leadership Theory

In the recent past, many school leaders have focused their energies on the managerial responsibilities of the school. This is an important job and cannot be neglected. Marzano et al. (2005) referred to this as *situational awareness*. Visibility is another responsibility from these authors that follows situational awareness. Effective school leaders need to be in frequent contact with all stakeholders of the school.

The dilemma that has arisen relates to school leaders spending too much time in management leadership and not enough time in instructional leadership. How do effective school leaders balance these key responsibilities? Can some areas of management be delegated to other leaders as *distributed leadership* (Elmore, 2000; Spillane & Scherer, 2004) suggests? Recent pressures from the federal government, states, local districts, and parents have been to encourage school leaders to be more of an instructional leader than a managerial leader.

Total quality management (Deming, 1986; Waldman, 1993) is a theory of leadership that suggests the qualities that effective school leaders need to provide the services of operations and management can be found within this theory. The five actions of effective leaders according to this theory are change agency, teamwork, continuous improvement, trust building, and eradication of short-term goals.

PSEL Standard 10: School Improvement

"Effective educational leaders act as agents of continuous improvement to promote each student's success and well-being."

The following 10 elements elaborate on the work necessary to meet this standard. Effective leaders (a) seek to make school more effective for students, teachers, staff, families, and the community; (b) use methods of continuous improvement to achieve the vision, fulfill the mission, and promote the core values of the school; (c) prepare the school and the community for improvement, promoting readiness, an imperative for improvement; instilling mutual commitment and accountability; and developing the knowledge, skills, and motivation to succeed in improvement; (d) engage others in an ongoing process of evidence-based inquiry, learning, strategic goal setting, planning implementation, and evaluation for continuous school and classroom improvement; (e) employ situationally appropriate strategies for improvement, including transformational and incremental, adaptive approaches, and attention to different phases of implementation; (f) assess and develop the capacity of staff to assess the value and applicability of emerging educational trends and the findings of research for the school and its improvement; (g) develop technologically appropriate systems of data collection, management, analysis, and use, connecting as needed to the district office and external partners for support in planning, implementation, monitoring, feedback, and evaluation; (h) adopt a systems perspective and promote coherence among improvement efforts and all aspects of school organization, programs, and services; (i) manage uncertainty, risk, competing initiatives, and politics of change with courage and perseverance, providing support and encouragement, and openly communicating the need for, process for, and outcomes of improvement efforts; and (j) develop and promote leadership among teachers and staff or inquiry, experimentation and innovation, and initiating and implementing improvement.

The Leadership Framework Domain 1: Leadership Competencies 1a, 1b, 1c, 1d, and 1e; Domain 2: Professional Learning and Growth Practices 2a, 2b, 2c, and 2d; Domain 3: Instructional Practices 3a, 3b, 3c, and 3d; and Domain 4: Management Competencies 4a, 4b, 4c, 4d, and 4e

The Leadership Framework promotes continuous school improvement by inviting effective school leaders to learn and practice the components and elements in each domain. Effective school leaders need to have leadership competencies, a deep reservoir of professional learning and growth activities, an understanding of student learning, and a repertoire of management competencies. This is the challenge of school leaders today.

Leadership Theory

DuFour and Marzano (2011) assert that schools can continuously improve if they become professional learning communities in which the adults work and learn together. Warwick (2015) advocates that, if schools adopted the continual improvement philosophy, they could improve by building staff collaboration that improves various internal systems. Both of these approaches are worth investigating in further detail.

This is *distributed leadership* (Elmore, 2000; Spillane & Scherer, 2004). By involving all stakeholders, effective school leaders are encouraging buy-in or common ownership. The work of continuous school improvement is not a one-man or one-woman leadership responsibility. It is the work of a community of educators who will do whatever it takes to ensure student learning and personal growth.

Summary

The purpose of this chapter is to connect the PSEL (2015) to *The Leadership Framework* and to the theories of effective educational leadership. The PSEL (2015) were unpacked and presented as meaningful practices of school leaders. These standards provided an outline of what effective leaders need to know and do.

Connections to *The Leadership Framework* added further depth to an understanding of effective school leadership. Leadership theories were connected to the PSEL (2015) and to *The Leadership Framework* as the foundational stepping-stones fostering deeper conversations about effective school leadership through the supportive process of supervision, evaluation, and professional learning for educational leaders.

Case Study

As the new superintendent of Durham School District #77, you wish to focus on the quality of leadership of the central office staff and in the school leadership teams of the five elementary schools, three middle schools, and one high school in the district. Create a three-year district-wide professional plan to address goals that all administrators in your district will work toward in terms of effective school leadership. Include the use of the PSEL (2015), *The Leadership Framework*, and theories of leadership.

Discussion Questions for Case Study

1. In *The Leadership Framework*, there are four domains, 18 components, and 90 elements. In which domains are you most proficient? In which domains is there need for growth or further experience?

2. Domain 2 of *The Leadership Framework* addresses professional learning and growth practices. What is your professional learning and growth plan for this year?

3. Domain 3 of *The Leadership Framework* focuses on instructional practices. How will you help align and support curriculum, instruction, assessment, and professional growth and learning with your teachers this year?

4. Domain 4 of *The Leadership Framework* asserts that effective school leaders have management competencies. How do you, as a leader, balance management with instructional leadership?

5. Evaluate the PSEL (2015). What did you learn from these expanded standards? How will these standards help you in your role as an educational leader?

6. Which leadership theories ground your experiences of leadership? How do you blend theory and practice?

Self-Assessment and Reflection

The Leadership Framework identifies and defines the work of effective school leaders. Leaders need to possess leadership competencies, a deep reservoir of professional learning and growth activities, an understanding of student learning, and a repertoire of management competencies. Evaluate yourself using *The Leadership Framework* (Appendix A) and the rubrics provided in chapter 2 and chapter 3. Develop two professional goals based on your self-assessment. You will further explore your goals in chapter 8.

References

Bass, B., & Avolio, B. (1994). *Improving organizational effectiveness through transformational leadership*. Thousand Oaks, CA: Sage.

Bolden, R., Gosling, J., Marturano, A., & Dennison, P. (2003). *A review of leadership theory and competency frameworks*. Exeter, UK: Center for Leadership Studies, University of Exeter.

Burns, J. (1978). *Leadership*. New York, NY: Harper & Row.

Cordeiro, P., and Cunningham, W. (2013). *Educational leadership: A bridge to improved practice*. (5th ed.). New York, NY: Pearson.

Cordeiro, P., & Monroe-Kolek, M. (1996). *Connecting school communities through educational partnerships*. New York, NY: Pearson.

Cotton, K. (2003). *Principals and student achievement: What the research says*. Alexandria, VA: Association of Supervision and Curriculum Development.

Council of Chief State School Officers (CCSSO) and the National Governors Association Center for Best Practices (NGA Center). (2015). The Common Core State Standards. Retrieved from http://www.corestandards.org/about-the-standards/

Deal, T., & Kennedy, A. (1999). *The new corporate cultures: Revitalizing the workplace after downsizing, mergers and reengineering*. New York, NY: Basic Books.

Deming, W. (1986). *Out of crisis*. Cambridge, MA: MIT Center for Advanced Engineering.

DuFour, R., & Marzano, R. (2011). *Leaders of learning: How district, school and classroom leaders improve student achievement*. Bloomington, IN: Solution Tree Press.

Elmore, R. (2000). *Building a new structure for school leadership*. New York, NY: Albert Shanker Institute.

Fullan, M., & Hargreaves, A. (1996). *What's worth fighting for in your school?* New York, NY: Teachers College Press.

Geneen, H. and Moscow, A. (1985). *Managing*. New York: Doubleday.

Greenleaf, R. (1977). *Servant leadership: A journey into the nature of legitimate power and greatness*. New York, NY: Paulist Press.

Gruenert, S., & Whitaker, T. (2015). *School culture rewired: How to define, assess and transform it*. Alexandria, VA: Association of Supervision and Curriculum Development.

Hargreaves, A., & Boyle, A. (2015). Uplifting leadership. *Educational Leadership*, 72(5), 42–47.

Hattie, J. (2015). High impact leadership. *Educational Leadership*, 72(5), 36–40.

Hersey, P., & Blanchard, K. (1982). *Management of organizational behavior: Utilizing human resources*. Englewood Cliffs, NJ: Prentice Hall.

Leithwood, K. (1994). Leadership for school restructuring. *Educational Administration Quarterly, 30*(4), 498–518.

Leithwood, K., & Riehl, C. (2003). *What we know about successful school leadership.* Philadelphia, PA: Laboratory for Student Success, Temple University.

Marzano, R., Waters, T., & McNulty, B. (2005). *School leadership that works: From research to results.* Alexandria, VA: Association of Supervision and Curriculum Development.

McTighe, J., & Wiggins, G. (2013). *Essential questions: Opening doors to student understanding.* Alexandria, VA: Association of Supervision and Curriculum Development.

National College for Teaching and Leadership. (2014). *Leadership framework for head teachers.* Retrieved from https://www.gov.uk/national-professional-qualification-for-senior-leadership-npqsl

National College for Teaching and Leadership. (2015). *Guidance: Develop the skills, knowledge and confidence you need to become a highly effective headteacher.* Retrieved from https://www.gov.uk/guidance/hational-professioal-qualitifcation-for-headship-npqh

National Policy Board for Educational Administration. (2015). *Professional standards for educational leaders 2015.* Reston, VA: Author.

Robinson, V., Lloyd, C., & Rowe, K. (2008). The impact of leadership on student outcomes: An analysis of the differential effects of leadership types. *Educational Administration Quarterly, 44*(5), 635–674.

Sergiovanni, T. (1992). *Moral leadership: Getting to the heart of school improvement.* San Francisco, CA: Jossey-Bass.

Sergiovanni, T. (1999). *Rethinking leadership.* Glenview, IL: Skylight.

Spears, L. (1995). *Reflections on leadership: How Robert K. Greenleaf's servant leadership influenced today's top management thinkers.* New York, NY: Wiley Press.

Spillane, J., & Sherer, J. (2004). *A distributed perspective on school leadership: Leadership practice as stretched over people and place.* The Distributive Leadership Study: Northwestern University.

Starratt, R. (1994). *Building an ethical school: A practical response to the moral crisis in schools.* London: Falmer Press.

Tableman, B., & Herron, A. (2004). School climate and learning. *BRIEFS, 31,* 1–10.

Tomal, D., Wilhite, R., Phillips, B., Sims, P., & Gibson, N. (2015). *Supervision and evaluation for learning and growth.* Lanham, MD: Rowman & Littlefield.

University of Tennessee Libraries Diversity Committee. (2015). *What is diversity?* Knoxville, TN: University Libraries, University of Tennessee, Knoxville. Retrieved from http://www.lib.utk.edu/diversity/definition/

Waldman, M. (1993). A theoretical consideration of leadership and TQM. *Leadership Quarterly, 4*(1), 65–79.

Warwick, R. (2015). *The challenge for school leaders: A new way of thinking about leadership.* Lanham, MD: Rowman & Littlefield.

CHAPTER SIX

The Diverse Roles of Leadership

If your actions inspire others to dream more, learn more, do more and become more, you are a leader.

—John Quincy Adams

Objectives

At the conclusion of this chapter you will be able to:

1. Compare and contrast the differences between management and leadership (PSEL 1, 2, 4, 5, 6, 8, 9; NELP 1, 2, 6).
2. Compare and contrast responsibilities of school leaders through the lens of each management and leadership (PSEL 1, 2, 5, 8, 9, 11; NELP 1, 2, 6).
3. Analyze roles and responsibilities of school leaders through the context and content of *The Leadership Framework* (PSEL 1, 2, 4, 5, 6, 8, 9, 11; NELP 1, 2, 6).
4. Integrate the use of *The Leadership Framework* in the development of a differentiated evaluation plan (PSEL 1, 2, 8, 9; NELP 1, 2, 3, 6).

Leadership and Management

The function of leadership has been questioned whether in business, government, or education. One aspect within the discussion of leadership has focused on the distinction between management, which educational administrators typically do with reasonable success, and leadership, which educational administrators often do not make a priority (Hord, 1992).

The literature communicates a wealth of information about the concepts of leadership and management, which are often confused. *Management* is concerned primarily with getting the work of the organization completed in an efficient and effective manner. Its focus is on the day-to-day functioning of the organization, giving primary attention to getting the job done (Lalonde, 2010). In contrast, *leadership* focuses on the future or what needs to be done. Its focus is on vision, empowerment, and achieving goals (Lalonde, 2010).

While the manager will direct the stakeholders to complete the required tasks the most efficient way, the leader tends to inspire or venture into new ways of doing things. Leadership is viewed to influence process, while management is seen as utilizing control (Catano & Stronge, 2007). The leader seeks to find new solutions to bring about improvement, while the manager seeks to assure that all participants remain on task and meet their required goals. The leader is concerned with understanding and changing beliefs and changing status quo. The manager, however, advocates stability and carries out his responsibilities by exercising authority to get the goals accomplished (Lunenburg, 2011).

Both leadership and management are important in the effective functioning of a school and district. Bennis and Nanus (2007) said, "Managers are people who do things right, while leaders are people who do the right thing." This phrase simply expresses the differences in the two functions in which administrators or executive personnel engage. One of the major contributions that a leader can make is to distinguish between these two important functions. The hectic and fast-paced obligations and expectations of an educational leader make it difficult to lose sight of whether or not they are doing the right thing.

One of the first researchers to compare and contrast the differences between management and leadership was Abraham Zalenik of Harvard University. In 1977, he published an article in which he shared his belief that both leaders and managers were important to organizations even though their contributions differed. Managers tend to focus their attention on completing tasks in an efficient and effective manner, whereas leaders were more focused on trying to understand the people in the organization and gain their trust. Managers tend to rely on authority to accomplish their tasks, whereas leaders tended to utilize persuasion and influence (Zalenik, 1977).

Leaders should be consistently asking the hard questions: Are we getting the best results possible? Where can we improve? Are there ethical issues involved? What knowledge and skills do we need to achieve the best results? How do we know if we are achieving the targeted goals (Kaser, Mundry, Stiles, & Loucks-Horsley, 2006, p. 49)?

Who Are School Leaders?

Based on the traditions, beliefs, and knowledge of leadership, it is easy to make the case that leadership is vital to the effectiveness of a school (Marzano, Waters, & McNulty, 2005, pp. 4–5). School superintendents, principals, and teachers are expected to instruct and manage to be effective leaders. These leaders face daily tension as they attempt to accomplish their instructional and managerial responsibilities within the constraints of time. Most leaders are passionate about being an instructional leader, yet they admit that they spend most of their time on managerial tasks (Cuban, 2010).

Effective school districts are those that acknowledge and embrace the knowledge, dispositions, skills, and practices of their leaders to best support both the leadership and managerial needs of the district and schools. School districts and individual schools need strong leadership. Managerial competencies are also imperative to the total workings of a successful school. The competencies detailed in Domain 4 of *The Leadership Framework* address the areas required of leaders to manage the district or building: adheres to personnel requirements, reports accurately and timely, upholds rules and regulations, practices and refines resourcefulness, and manages effectively.

Roles and Responsibilities of School Leaders

It is important for districts and schools to be mindful of the different roles and responsibilities of their leaders. The responsibilities and expectations of the job may include leadership attributes as well as managerial tasks. As a job description is developed, the type of attributes, leadership, and management should be aligned with the goals of the position. Subsequently, the person selected for each position should be well aware of the expectations of the job and how he or she will be expected to provide evidence of accomplishment and achievement.

The following are examples of job responsibilities of a superintendent, assistant superintendent for teaching and learning, assistant superintendent of human resources, assistant superintendent of finance and operations, and principal. The noted responsibilities do not reflect a comprehensive job description but are a few examples of common expectations often included for these positions. These five examples are also not the only leadership positions in a school district but are representative of common areas of responsibility. Each is aligned to a component of *The Leadership Framework*. As this is meant to be a sample, every component of *The Leadership Framework* may not have a job responsibility aligned to it.

The *superintendent of schools* or *chief executive officer* (CEO) is essentially the face of the district. The superintendent is responsible for the success of a district and most assuredly held responsible when there are failures. The superintendent sets the direction and tone while responding to the many competing demands of the board of education, administrators, teachers, parents, students, and the community. The superintendent must possess a unique skill set in order to be effective. Organized by *The Leadership Framework*, examples of responsibilities may include:

Domain 1: Leadership Competencies
1a. Establishes a solid foundation
- Facilitates the development of a strategic plan for the ongoing improvement of the district.
- Assumes the responsibility for the development of the mission, vision, and goals for the district.

1b. Builds shared leadership
- Delegates authority to staff members and work teams as appropriate.

1c. Initiates effective communication
- Communicates effectively through written and spoken word.
- Prepares agenda for board meetings, which includes recommendations for board action, information, and reports needed to ensure the making of informed decisions.
- Assumes responsibility for keeping the board of education informed of the ongoing events and issues of the school district.
- Accepts responsibility for news releases and other items of public interest emanating from all district employees that pertain to educational matters, policies, procedures, school-related incidents, and events.

1d. Adheres to a moral compass
- Exercises good judgment in seeking information and counsel, analyzing facts and situations and arriving at decisions.

1e. Promotes a positive school culture
- Develops and maintains positive relationships with students, parents, community, and local businesses.

Domain 2: Professional Learning and Growth Practices
2b. Fosters and facilitates continual improvement
- Guides the board of education in the development of new district policy and the review and revision of old policy.

Domain 4: Management competencies
4a. Adheres to personnel requirements
- Supervises and evaluates district-level administration.
4c. Upholds rules and regulations
- Provides effective voice for the district with local, state, and federal agencies.
- Maintains positive relationships with the legislature relating to public education.
4d. Practices and refines resourcefulness
- Builds relationships with other school districts to allow for the exchange of ideas and best practice.
- Builds and maintains positive relationships with the local media.
- Provides overall direction to interdistrict cooperatives in special education, vocational education, and alternative education.
4e. Manages effectively
- Evaluates the needs of the district and makes recommendations for building improvements and potential bond issues.
- Exercises general supervision and control over all aspects of the district operations.

An *assistant superintendent for teaching and learning*, also often referred to as *assistant superintendent of curriculum and instruction* or *assistant superintendent of teaching and learning*, is generally responsible for the oversight of the development, implementation, and monitoring of all instructional programs and services. Organized by *The Leadership Framework*, examples of responsibilities may include:

Domain 1: Leadership Competencies
1a. Establishes a solid foundation
- Develops annual goals and action planning for the teaching and learning program.

1c. Initiates effective communication
- Coordinates and articulates the curricular expectations among and between grade levels.

Domain 2: Professional Learning and Growth Practices
2a. Demonstrates competence as an educational leader
- Oversees the planning, development, and implementation of professional learning for professional and administrative staff in the area of teaching and learning.
- Maintains a high level of competence in the field of education, remaining current in issues related to areas of responsibility.

2b. Fosters and facilitates continual improvement
- Monitors and assesses programs and identifies areas in need of improvement.

Domain 3: Instructional Practices
3a. Champions and supports curriculum development
- Ensures a viable and rigorous curriculum for all grade levels and courses.
- Assumes responsibility for the implementation of curriculum aligned with state frameworks, student and teacher performance objectives, and curriculum standards and proficiencies in all courses.
- Orchestrates the evaluation of instructional materials, including texts, digital resources, and other instructional materials.

3b. Advocates for instruction that supports the needs of all learners
- Serves on district committees and participates in district activities in conjunction with teaching and learning.
- Provides leadership in developing plans for instructional research, pilot studies for curriculum, instruction, technology, and new courses of study.

3c. Analyzes assessments
- Ensures that the use of data is integral in the evaluation and development of recommendations for all aspects of teaching and learning.

Domain 4: Management Competencies
4a. Adheres to personnel requirements
- Supervises and evaluates curriculum coordinators and directors in compliance with local and state policies and procedures.

4b. Reports accurately and timely
- Assists in the creation of all reports, records, and other compliance documents as required by the board of education, state board of education, and the federal government.

4c. Upholds rules and regulations
- Supervises the implementation of the educational and instructional programs in compliance with local, state, and federal regulations and within the guidelines of the district's collective bargaining agreement.

4d. Practices and refines resourcefulness
- Seeks and applies for appropriate competitive grants to support the area of teaching and learning.
- Provides input in the development of the budget, including staffing, instructional materials and resources, and professional learning.
- Develops, monitors, and maintains federal and competitive grant budgets.

An *assistant superintendent for human resources* is responsible for ensuring a high-quality work force that has the capacity to successfully meet the diverse needs of students, parents, and the community. This position requires a vast amount of human resource knowledge, skill, and organizational talents in order to be effective. Critical to the success in this role is the planning, coordinating, and participating in the recruitment and retainment of personnel. Organized by *The Leadership Framework*, examples of responsibilities may include:

Domain 1: Leadership Competencies
1b. Builds shared leadership
- Attempts to retain a workforce of highly competent and effective professionals.

1c. Initiates effective communication
- Prepares and delivers written and oral presentations on management issues to the board of education.
- Maintains clearly stated policies, regulations, and procedures related to the function, rights, and responsibilities of the staff
- Ensures that those directly affected by personnel policies have knowledge of relevant policies and procedures.

1d. Adheres to a moral compass
- Strives to employ persons from various ethnic diversities and institutions of learning.

Domain 2: Professional Learning and Growth Practices
2c. Promotes professional learning and growth
- Maintains a high level of competence in the field of human resource management.

Domain 4: Management Competencies

4a. Adheres to personnel requirements

- Monitors personnel policies.
- Coordinates employee performance evaluation procedures.
- Plans, coordinates, and participates in the recruitment of personnel.
- Recommends certified and classified candidates to the superintendent on the basis of their qualifications for potential hiring.

4b. Reports accurately and timely

- Monitors student enrollment projections and develops projections for staffing needs.

4c. Upholds rules and regulations

- Makes personnel decisions based on professionally sound, documented personnel policies and procedures.
- Administers employee benefits and insurance.
- Administers provisions of district procedures concerning transfers, discipline, leaves of absence, resignations, retirement, vacations, stipends, and absences.
- Directs, plans, and participates in ensuring compliance with all applicable federal and state law as it relates to personnel.
- Acts as a liaison between the school district and union leadership.

An *assistant superintendent for finance and operations* is primarily responsible for developing and maintaining a viable school budget. School finance is not an exact science. It is a complicated formula that changes from year to year, especially in the realm of public education (Meador, 2018). The management and distribution of funds should be an impetus for thoughtful and meaningful decision-making in the school district, especially in times of deficits. Recommending budget cuts may have an impact on the quality of education the district provides. Organized by *The Leadership Framework*, examples of responsibilities may include:

Domain 4: Management Competencies

4b. Reports accurately and timely

- Prepares annual budget for the school district and serves as representative of the superintendent in controlling the adopted budget.
- Audits all expense accounts, bills, contracts, and other claims prior to submitting for approval.
- Files real estate deeds and abstracts, titles to motor vehicles, contractual agreements, and other official documents involved in business transactions.

4c. Upholds rules and regulations
- Prepares financial, business, and facility reports for the superintendent, school board, and state and federal agencies.
- Assumes responsibility for the collection of all funds due the district and deposits these funds in the manner prescribed by law.
- Disburses district funds in accordance with board policy, the adopted school budget, and state and federal law.
- Administers the payroll system for district employees.
- Serves as purchasing agent for the district in accordance with approved board policy.

4d. Practices and refines resourcefulness
- Assists the superintendent and staff to analyze financial and educational issues to develop solutions to problems that ultimately improve daily operations.
- Ensures the investment of district funds, with maximization of investment revenue while maintaining the safety of district funds as the priority.

4e. Manages effectively
- Aligns district resources with district goals and priorities through budget development and management.
- Supervises construction projects and major district repairs.
- Administers the board's policy on the use of school properties by non-school agencies.
- Maintains adequate inventories of all physical properties of the district.

The role of the school *principal* is a complex one at best. Although responsibilities vary by locality, school composition, and school size, the principal is primarily responsible for administering all aspects of a school's operation (Lunenburg, 2010).

For much of the past century, the typical role of the school principal was to serve as the manager-in-chief, an administrator who makes sure the boilers worked, buses ran on time, and new teachers were hired and placed in classrooms. Certainly, the principal disciplined children who misbehaved and awarded certificates to those with perfect attendance, but to most students the person running the school was usually a shadowy figure, someone lurking on the periphery of their day-to-day educational lives (DuBois, 2012).

In the wake of school reform during the past decade, the role of the principal has changed dramatically. The major driver for this shift was the emergence of massive accountability that holds principals and schools responsible for student outcomes as evidenced in achievement scores. Organized by *The Leadership Framework*, examples of responsibilities may include:

Domain 1: Leadership Competencies
1a. Establishes a solid foundation
- Supports the strategic plan of the district.
- Maintains visibility with students, teachers, parents, and community.
- Develops and maintains a professional and respectful rapport with students and staff.

1c. Initiates effective communication
- Communicates effectively with staff, students, parents, and district to encourage ongoing and open discussion.
- Communicates regularly with parents to create a cooperative relationship to support the student at school.
- Uses appropriate written and oral skills when communicating with students, staff, and community.

1e. Promotes a positive school culture
- Ensures a safe, orderly environment that encourages students to take responsibility for behavior and encourages positive climate.
- Assumes responsibility for the health, safety, and welfare of students, staff, and visitors.
- Develops and implements clearly understood procedures and protocols for emergencies and disasters.

Domain 2: Professional Learning and Growth Practices
2a. Demonstrates competence as an educational leader
- Models effective instructional strategies to support the instructional practices and high expectations for student engagement.

Domain 3: Instructional Practices
3a. Champions and supports curriculum development
- Establishes procedures for the evaluation and selection of instructional support materials and equipment.

3b. Advocates for instruction that supports the needs of all learners
- Identifies intellectual, physical, social, and emotional needs affecting students' success in school.
- Aligns the goals of the school to support district initiatives and promote student achievement.
- Maintains high standards and expectations for the academic achievement of all students.

3c. Analyzes assessments
- Plans appropriately and implements accordingly for all state and local assessments.
- Ensures that the use of data is integral in the evaluation and development of recommendations for all aspects of student achievement and teacher accountability.
- Supervises the instructional programs of the school on a regular basis to ensure the appropriate use of instructional strategies and materials consistent with research and best practice.

3d. Incorporates technology to enhance learning
- Encourages the use of technology to support student learning and instructional delivery.

Domain 4: Management Competencies
4a. Adheres to personnel requirements
- Supervises and evaluates all staff in accordance with district procedures and protocol.

4b. Reports accurately and timely
- Maintains accurate records and reports as required by the district and state.

4e. Manages effectively
- Manages, evaluates, and supervises effective procedures for the operation and functioning of the school.

Differentiation of Leaders' Roles

The different job descriptions of the district and school leaders make up a complex interwoven web of roles, responsibilities, and outcomes all focusing on a highly effective school system and subsequently high-achieving students. As different as each of the roles may be, so should the supervision and evaluation practices of each role. *The Leadership Framework* provides a structure for any role in the school district to use the same rubric in an individualized manner to provide necessary *differentiation*.

The roles and responsibilities of the superintendent are primarily aligned in Domain 1: Leadership Competencies and Domain 4: Management Competencies. The assistant superintendent for teaching and learning is highly aligned in Domain 2: Professional Learning and Growth Practices and Domain 3: Instructional Practices. The roles and responsibilities of the assistant superintendent for finance and operations are almost entirely aligned with Domain 4: Management Competencies.

The principal's role is interwoven within all four domains. Even though each position may focus on different components of *The Leadership Framework*, the organization has the capacity to use the same evaluation and supervision rubric, use common language when discussing improvement practices, and strive for movement on the continuum toward a distinguished rating.

Summary

School districts and schools need strong leaders and managers to lead effectively. The differences between leaders and managers should be acknowledged and their responsibilities in the workplace should be aligned accordingly. Good leaders are not necessarily good managers, and good managers are not necessarily good leaders (Lunenburg, 2011). It is incumbent upon the school district to ensure that all school personnel are well qualified for the roles and responsibilities for which they are hired.

The Leadership Framework may be used for supervision and evaluation of school leadership. By aligning the responsibilities of the position to *The Leadership Framework*, the individual is able to reflect on performance, evaluate outcomes, and develop a professional growth and learning plan. Additionally, *The Leadership Framework* can be used as a guide for the preparation of new leadership, a road map for novice leadership, and a tool to guide the enhancement of knowledge, skills, dispositions, and practices of veteran leadership.

Case Study

It is April 15, and Dr. John Standard has just been appointed as the new superintendent of Ridgeway Community School District beginning the upcoming school year. His previous superintendent's experience included noted successes in two different districts, both of which had been very low achieving with highly diverse populations. During his tenure in those districts, substantial academic gains were made, and school improvement plans were developed and implemented to continue ongoing positive change.

Ridgeway Community School District is anxious to have Dr. Standard take over the leadership of its schools in hopes of substantial and needed improvement. Ridgeway's schools have been identified as *turnaround*, and the first task Dr. Standard needs to address is the replacement of all the principals. The board of education has directed Dr. Standard to have the hiring of principals completed no later than June 15.

Discussion Questions

1. Review the 25 categories of principal behaviors (Cotton, 2003) and the 21 responsibilities of a school leader (Marzano et al., 2005) in Table 4.3. Which categories and responsibilities do you believe are important to include in the job descriptions for the new principals?
2. How might you begin the search for the new principals with the specific knowledge, skills, dispositions, and practices that align with the newly developed job description?
3. Which stakeholders do you believe should have involvement in the hiring process? What would their roles include?
4. Using *The Leadership Framework*, create an evaluation system for the new principals that targets the expected knowledge, skills, dispositions, and practices that are expected to be evidenced in their new role.
5. Align each of the components of the principal's job description to *The Leadership Framework*.
6. Develop a plan to share the alignment of *The Leadership Framework* and evaluation timeline with the principals before the beginning of the school year.

Self-Assessment and Reflection

Given what you know about the alignment of *The Leadership Framework* and the components of an educational job description, develop an evaluation system for the assistant superintendent of information/data services or director of technology of your school. What knowledge, skills, dispositions, and practices should the candidate possess for this position? Include examples from each of *The Leadership Framework* domains: Leadership Competencies, Professional Learning and Growth Practices, Instructional Practices, and Management. How will you use *The Leadership Framework* to guide the professional learning and evaluation of this important district-level position?

References

Bennis, W. G. (1989). Managing the dream: Leadership in the 21st century. *Journal of Organizational Change Management, 2*, 7.

Catano, N., & Stronge, J. H. (2007). What do we expect of school principals? Congruence between principal evaluation and performance standards. *International Journal of Leadership in Education, 10*(4), 379–399. doi:10.1080/13603120701381782

Cotton, K. (2003). *Principals and student achievement: What the research says.* Alexandria, VA: Association of Supervision and Curriculum Development.

Cuban, L. (2010). *Principals as instructional leaders—again and again.* Retrieved from https://larrycuban.wordpress.com/2010/12/01/principals-as-instructional-leaders-again-and-again/

DuBois, L. (2012). *Principals' leadership and leadership principles.* Retrieved from https://news.vanderbilt.edu/2023/07/05/principals-leadership-and-leadership-principles-2/

Hord, S. M. (1992). *Facilitative leadership: The imperative for change.* Austin, TX: Southwest Educational Development Laboratory.

Kaser, J., Mundry, S., Stiles, K., & Loucks-Horsley, S. (2006). *Leading every day: 124 actions for effective leadership.* Thousand Oaks, CA: Sage.

Lalonde, M. T. (2010). Early childhood education is leadership. *The Early Childhood Educator, 25*(2), p. 2.

Lunenburg, F. C. (2010). The principal and the school: What do principals do? *National Forum of Educational Administration and Supervision Journal, 27,* 1–9.

Lunenburg, F. C. (2011). Leadership versus management: A key—at least in theory. *International Journal of Management, Business, and Administration, 14*(1).

Marzano, R., Waters, T., & McNulty, B. (2005). *School leadership that works: From research to results.* Alexandria, VA: Association of Supervision and Curriculum Development, 42–43.

Meador, D. (2018, July 10). Examining the role of an effective school superintendent. Retrieved from http://teaching.about.com/od/admin/a/Superintendent-Of-Schools.htm

Zalenik, A. (1977). Managers and leaders: Are they different? *Harvard Business Review, 55*(5), 67–78.

∽

CHAPTER SEVEN

Professional Learning to Enhance Effective Leadership

Leadership and learning are indispensable to each other.

—John F. Kennedy

Objectives

At the conclusion of this chapter you will be able to:

1. Analyze the components of professional learning (PSEL 1, 2, 3, 4, 5, 6, 7, 10; NELP 1, 2, 3, 4, 7).
2. Critique and recommend models of professional learning (PSEL 2, 3, 4, 6, 7; NELP 2, 3, 4, 7).
3. Compare and contrast professional learning and professional development (PSEL 2, 3, 4, 6, 7; NELP 2, 3, 4, 7).
4. Articulate the alignment of professional learning to district and school goals (PSEL 1, 2, 3, 4, 5, 6, 7, 10; NELP 1, 2, 3, 4, 5, 6, 7).
5. Integrate *The Leadership Framework* in the design of a professional learning plan (PSEL 1, 2, 3, 4, 7, 10; NELP 1, 2, 3, 4, 5, 6, 7).

What Is Professional Learning?

Professional learning is an ongoing process, not an event. It is not a one-time activity or workshop that fulfills a requirement for certification or compliance. Professional learning is based on the belief that learning is a continual process. The main purpose of professional learning is to improve educator practice and student achievement. Professional learning is the essential component for schools to strengthen their educational workforce through acquisition of new knowledge and skills, increased abilities, reflection on change, and focus on student learning. Continuous improvement of individuals, schools, and school systems depends on high-quality professional learning.

The Leadership Framework supports the work of *Learning Forward* and the standards for professional learning. Implicit in the standards are several prerequisites for effective professional learning. Without these prerequisites, meaningful and effective professional learning may not be possible (Learning Forward, 2011). Researchers found that although 90 percent of teachers reported participating in professional development, most participants also reported that it was totally useless (Darling-Hammond et al., 2009).

Educators' commitment to students—*all* students—is the foundation of effective professional learning. Each educator involved in professional learning comes to the experience ready to learn. Because experience levels and use of practice among educators differ, professional learning can foster collaborative inquiry and learning that enhances individual and collective performance. Like all learners, educators learn in different ways and at different rates (Learning Forward, 2011, p. 15).

Subsequently, all educators—especially leaders—must be committed to engaging in continuous professional improvement to deepen their knowledge and expand their skills and practices. They must be ready to engage with one another to access new knowledge, skills, dispositions, and practices. In addition, they will be more receptive to new learning when it is directly aligned with their professional goals and daily responsibilities.

Each individual must be engaged in ongoing, timely, focused, and high-quality professional learning. The professional learning should be differentiated to meet the learning styles and needs of each learner or educator. Stephanie Hirsh, executive director of Learning Forward, stated, "Professional learning—when it's systemic, where it's being done as a sustained process inside a school, when it's ongoing, experiential, collaborative, and connected to students—is more powerful than any video, presentation, or catalogue of workshops" (as cited in Walker, 2013, p. 4).

Professional development models can be placed in three broad categories: *standardized, site based,* or *self-directed. Standardized* refers to professional development and learning presented to the whole group or whole school. It has benefits: it is cost effective, all faculty and staff receive the same information, new or common knowledge can be disseminated quickly, and it can create or strengthen bonds among participants. Among its drawbacks are it is a one-shot approach rather than long term and often doesn't include follow-up or support. Unless the new concept or skill is put into practice immediately following the session, it is unlikely to be used, remembered, or met with fidelity.

Another drawback is lack of differentiation, so participants may not view information as relevant or meaningful. Too, participants may be in and out of the session. It is not uncommon for administrators to run to the office, take a call, or be called out for a crisis. As a whole, participants are often observed texting, e-mailing, reading, or doing other activities that divide their attention. This model of professional development includes institute days at the beginning of the year or professional development days throughout the school year. Information may be disseminated to the masses in different ways, including from a guest speaker, digital video clip, webinar, or distance learning.

Site-based professional development refers to a particular group or portion of the staff and has the capacity to promote long-term, profound, and intense learning that can change instructional methods, improve knowledge of educational programs, and subsequently improve student learning. Its benefits are it fits the group members' needs and is relevant to their placements; it builds community, meets local needs, and is sustainable.

Among the drawbacks are creating time within the schedule to use site-based professional development effectively and limited group resources or expertise. Examples of site-based development are professional learning communities, curriculum development, instructional planning, data analysis, facilitated group discussions, examining student work, assessing instructional materials, or working with teachers on professional development plans for license renewal. Educators create an environment that fosters mutual cooperation, emotional support, and personal growth as they work together to achieve what they cannot accomplish alone (DuFour & Eaker, 1998).

Self-directed professional development refers to the needs and interests of an individual faculty or staff member. Its benefits are a high level of flexibility and opportunity. Other of its strengths are it is of interest to the individual, and individuals who are engaging in professional growth not only affect their own students but also teams (grade level, content area, department) and colleagues. They often inspire others to embrace professional growth.

Some drawbacks include participants must be autonomous and self-motivated and, therefore, may have a high level of attrition. Self-directed professional development includes coursework for a terminal degree, distance learning, case studies, consortiums, action research, interviewing a colleague, coaching, mentoring, observations, site visits, reflective journaling, or modular exercises on the computer, such as the State of Illinois' Performance Evaluation Reform Act (PERA) training.

Guiding the process, the standards for professional learning (Learning Forward, 2011) delineate the conditions, processes, and content of professional learning to support continuous improvement of leadership, teaching, and student learning. These standards are the cornerstone of continuous professional learning for the effective leader. They are summarized in textbox 7.1.

Textbox 7.1. Standards for Professional Learning. Learning Forward, 2011.

Learning Communities: Professional learning that increases educator effectiveness and results for all students occurs within learning communities committed to continuous improvement, collective responsibility, and goal alignment.

Leadership: Professional learning that increases educator effectiveness and results for all students requires skillful leaders who develop capacity, advocate, and create support systems for professional learning.

Resources: Professional learning that increases educator effectiveness and results for all students requires prioritizing, monitoring, and coordinating resources for educator learning.

Learning Designs: Professional learning that increases educator effectiveness and results for all students integrates theories, research, and models of human learning to achieve its intended outcomes.

Data: Professional learning that increases educator effectiveness and results for all students uses a variety of sources and types of student, educator, and system data to plan, assess, and evaluate professional learning.

Implementation: Professional learning that increases educator effectiveness and results for all students applies research on change and sustains support for implementation of professional learning for long-term change.

Outcomes: Professional learning that increases educator effectiveness and results for all students aligns its outcomes with educator performance and student curriculum standards.

Professional Learning: Opportunities for Choice

No one model covers all professional learning. The beauty of the endeavor is that there are multiple ways to learn and as many different opportunities to achieve identified goals. Each individual may accomplish them in a different manner. The opportunities for professional learning are as vast as the number of participants and the goals to be achieved. The following will differentiate among the varieties of the most common professional learning models.

A professional learning community (PLC) "is an ongoing process in which educators work collaboratively in recurring cycles of collective inquiry and action research to achieve better results for the students they serve" (DuFour, DuFour, Eaker, & Many, 2010, p. 11). The sole focus of the professional learning community is job-embedded learning for educators to promote student achievement.

In order for a professional learning community to be effective, three components must be evident. First, the PLC must accept the goal of a high level of learning for all students. Second, the PLC can achieve a high level of learning only if the work is completed within a collaborative culture. Finally, assessment of the effectiveness of a high level of learning is based on results, rather than intentions.

In professional learning communities, teams are often built around shared roles or responsibilities. For example, a school leader may be in a particular group of colleagues who wish to focus on understanding content and various instructional strategies being used in the delivery of the curriculum. They may evaluate their current curriculum to ensure a deeper understanding of the content, alignment, and assessment of the current program.

Additionally, they may observe in classrooms to note the implementation of the instructional strategies to support the instruction. Together they will analyze the collected data and discuss the findings. Four questions (Solution Tree, 2007) help assess or monitor the intended outcome of the current goal and then assist in framing a new focused area for the PLC to engage in study:

1. What should students know and be able to do as a result of this course, class, or grade level?
2. How will we know that the students are not learning?
3. How do we respond when students do not learn?
4. How do we respond when students learn more?

A professional learning community is a powerful way of working together that can have a profound impact on the practices of the entire school community. When implemented with fidelity, it promotes three ideas: focus on learning, collaboration, and results. The focus is on learning, not teaching—not only for the students but equally for the leaders who set direction. Most importantly, the PLC participants hold themselves accountable for the results that will drive ongoing personal and continual academic improvement (DuFour, Eaker, & DuFour, 2005, p. 42). Textbox 7.2 summarizes attributes of professional learning communities.

Textbox 7.2. Attributes of Professional Learning Communities

- Supportive and shared leadership
- Collective creativity
- Shared values and vision
- Supportive conditions
- Shared personal practice

Workshops and *seminars* are structured professional learning opportunities for leaders to learn from facilitators, educational experts, or peers with specialized expertise. Generally, a workshop is a single event or sometimes a series of work sessions that focus on a defined area of study. This type of learning opportunity may be of great value to the leader. As the topic homes in on a specified educational area, the new learning is focused toward the targeted goal. Also, this format often involves participants practicing their new skills and learning in a controlled setting.

Examples of workshops may include data collection and analysis for the improvement of student learning (Domain 3a), use of technology as a tool for effective school management (Domain 4b), understanding of curriculum standards and the alignment to what is taught (Domain 3b), and collaborative leadership strategies for school improvement (Domain 2b). As noted, these workshops align with the leadership framework elements. It is critical to choose a workshop description that best aligns with the needs of the leader in order to maximize the use of time and resources.

Seminars, or conferences, are similar to workshops, but they usually feature one or more subject area experts delivering information primarily via lecture and panel discussions. If the scope of the material is focused, then it could also be aligned with the leadership framework elements.

For example, the National Association of Elementary School Principals (NAESP) hosted a conference with sessions focused on mentoring (Domain 2a), growing diversity (Domain 1e), balanced leadership (Domain 1b), and moving a school from ordinary to extraordinary (Domain 2b). Blogs on their website include changing culture (Domain 1e) and Elementary and Secondary Education Act (ESEA) reauthorization bills (Domain 4c). The School Superintendents Association (AASA) also provided a two-day institute on college and career readiness (Domain 3b) and a three-day conference on transformational leadership focused on leading change, promoting innovation, and handling complexity (Domain 1a).

A *book study* is another model for professional learning. A book study is a conversation intended to stretch thinking and influence practice. The advantages of a book study include providing opportunities for collaboration with colleagues and affording flexible scheduling for meeting times. Again, a group of school leaders may come together to engage in critical reading, reflection, and application of the content of a specific book. For example, prior to implementing professional learning communities, you will want to engage faculty and staff in professional development. Although this may include *standardized* professional development with a speaker who addresses the whole staff, it may also include site-based professional development, such as a book study.

Purchasing a common text, providing a schedule that outlines dates with chapters to read for that meeting, encouraging faculty and staff to make reactive notations and reflective passages, providing guided questions for a group leader to follow, and actively monitoring group progress (including answering or collectively investigating questions posed) are all opportunities a book study presents. It can be followed with individualized professional development through further investigation and learning of the topic through coursework or attendance at an off-site workshop directly related to the study.

A book study may be used for *site-based* professional development where a portion of the staff identifies an area of interest and collectively chooses a book. Participation in the group should be voluntary, increasing the likelihood of the participants' active involvement. Leadership or facilitation of the book study group should be a shared responsibility.

District leaders may use a book study to provide a teacher or leader a *self-directed* opportunity to grow in an area of deficiency or weakness. In this case, the choice of book should be matched with the intended new learning as dictated by the effective leaders' goal for improvement or learning.

The assessment or monitoring of a book study is based on implementing new or developed learning. Evidence of implementation needs to be documented and specific. The following questions may be asked to determine effectiveness:

- How has this new learning been shared?
- What evidence of implementation has the effective leader provided?

- What data will be used to assess the effectiveness of the book study?
- What are the next steps toward goal attainment if the goal is not met?

Textbox 7.3 summarizes characteristics of effective book study groups.

Textbox 7.3. Characteristics of Effective Book Study Groups

- Involve participants in the decision-making process regarding content and group norms
- Include rituals and celebrations
- Determine norms and procedures as a group
- Avoid assuming certain participants are experts (all are here to learn)
- Consider the book study group a time for learning and reflective participation

---

Effective leaders may participate in *formalized coursework* offered by a university or college as an option for professional learning and growth. Coursework is not only academically healthy for the individual, but it also provides a structured format to assess current skill levels. For some in school leadership positions, it is incumbent upon the leader to advance his or her knowledge base in curricular development and alignment, technology integration, and/or data management, all of which have come to the forefront in recent years.

Formalized courses provide some advantages: structure, learning objectives, a conceptual framework, and access to the most current academic and practitioner scholarship. Further, they give school districts a way to measure the ability of their school leaders when they participate in a learning model with other colleagues from a variety of school communities and leadership responsibilities. The immersion of school leaders in formalized professional learning delivers a message to the community that staff members are continually upgrading their skills and applying new knowledge for the growth and improvement of student learning.

Such coursework can eventually lead to an advanced degree or certification with a specific focus on a targeted learning area—for example, reading specialist, curriculum director, or special education administrator. The variety of coursework available today includes face-to-face in-class participation, online learning through a cohort configuration that provides a more flexible format, or a hybrid that many universities or colleges provide. Personal learning styles, time constraints, cost, and professional goals will dictate which approach and educational venue is most appropriate for the leader to pursue.

Mentoring models are designed to promote professional learning by linking a leader with a mentor who will focus on his overall development. Mentoring is transformational and involves much more than simply acquiring a specific skill or knowledge. Mentoring is about building a relationship, both professional and personal (Management Mentors, 2013, p. 1).

Mentoring is influencing somebody by virtue of one's manners and expertise. A mentor is person focused. A mentor is like a sounding board: he can give advice and encourage the leader to discuss and clarify his path of behavior and expected outcome. The context does not have specific performance objectives. If mentoring is used as a professional learning model, the leader might use the leadership framework to identify specific goals or targeted areas for professional learning and growth.

Mentoring should be considered long term. It requires time for both participants to learn about one another and build a climate of trust that creates an environment in which the leader can feel secure in sharing the real issues that affect his success. Once trust is achieved, mentoring truly begins. For mentoring relationships to be successful, a mentoring program should be at least a year in duration and, ideally, continue longer.

Mentoring may be difficult to quantify. Mentoring is about relationships, so it is important to monitor the focused goals in the professional learning and growth plan. It is critical to determine how evidence and data will be collected and reported in order to demonstrate growth and learning.

When a professional learning and growth plan is developed, it may be determined that using a *coach* is the best model for goal attainment. The coach focuses impartially on improvement in behavior. *Coaching* is teaching somebody by virtue of one's experience. Coaching provides direct professional learning benefits to the leader and translates into student academic improvement. Kay Psencik, a leadership coach and author of *The Coach's Craft: Powerful Practices to Support School Leaders* (2011), defines coaching as "just-in-time, personalized support" (p. 30).

"Coaching, in its pure definition, is a person in relationship with the *coachee* in a way that the coach is able to ask strategic, focused questions that lead the coachee to learn and to make decisions for themselves," Psencik said. "The coach is honing the skills of the coaches so they are strong leaders" (p. 30).

It is important to note the significant difference between *evaluation* and *coaching*. A *coach* should approach the work with the leader as a process of inquiry. Coaching as inquiry suggests the use of thoughtful focused questions that promote self-assessment and reflection, as opposed to an investigation to assign blame (Carter, 2015). The intent of coaching as inquiry is to help the leader think about what he knows to be true and what questions, desires, and concerns he has in regard to aspects of work and performance. The values, personal and professional experiences, and disposition of the leader influence his thoughts and actions.

It is the coach's responsibility to frame the discussion in a mutually respectful dialogue focused on the desired outcomes and goal attainment. *Evaluation* is an assessment of the leader's work and attributes. Ongoing discussions with the coach should provide feedback on the work toward the desired outcome. Using the leadership framework as a guide, feedback can be aligned directly to areas identified with the specific behaviors and attributes within the rubric. Psencik (2011) suggests that educational leaders should look for coaches with proven achievement and the personal attributes that make a good coach; she has identified the following attributes to determine the compatibility between coach and leader:

- Self-awareness: What drives the coach? What inspires him?
- Honesty: How does what the coach thinks, does, and says align with his stated values?
- Sincerity: How do the coach's actions reflect his stated intentions?
- Competence: How credible is the coach?
- Reliability: Does the coach keep his promises?
- Intentionality: Is the coach interested in the leader and what he has to say? (pp. 89–92)

Peer teaching among leaders as an option is often overlooked. Learning is a social act, one deepened when adults are able to learn from one another. DuFour (1991) notes that peer learning can be an integral component of professional learning. Joyce and Showers (1995) echo that teamwork and partnering are needed to support new learning. The simple focus of working with others allows for the sharing of responsibilities and tasks as well as the reinforcement of social skills. Powerful leader education and learning is more than a matter of learning and practicing techniques and best practices; it involves engagement with others in debate of challenges, issues, and accomplishments.

Training or Professional Learning

Long gone are the days of professional development requirements being fulfilled by after-school workshops or hiring an expert to come to the school to train the educators in the current program du jour. Effective professional learning is characterized now by deliberate and thoughtful consideration of the existing needs, knowledge and beliefs, contexts, goals, and critical issues to inform the selection and combination of learning models (Kaser, Mundry, Stiles, & Loucks-Horsley, 2006, p. 186).

According to Reeves (2010), "The term *train* disturbs educators for a variety of reasons. Monkeys are trained, they say, and professionals are developed. Nevertheless, the term remains in active use in many school systems to refer to methods used to change the behavior of children and teachers" (p. 85). Further, he points to the *Shorter Oxford English Dictionary* definitions that validate the negative context with the term *train*. As a verb, the first definition is to draw or pull along; drag, haul. As a transitive verb it means drag out, protract, spin out; spend or pass time slowly or tediously. "Is it possible that the Oxford etymologists were participants in a recent staff development training?" (Reeves, 2010, p. 85).

It should be the goal of all educators to ensure that professional learning is worthwhile and engaging rather than drawn out and tedious. That said, the use of training in professional learning has a limited purpose. Training should be considered as a short-term commitment. Training sessions are often a single session for the purpose of learning how to do something.

Examples include a session with a technology expert demonstrating how to access the new e-mail or data management software (Domain 1c). The assistant superintendent for teaching and learning may train leaders on the techniques to access student data from the district data warehouse (Domain 3b). The director of operations may teach leaders the details and implementation of the building security system (Domain 4e). All of these examples have merit; to be effective, the leader needs to know that content. These elements of the leadership framework would certainly be supported by a training session or two.

The majority of the components and elements of the leadership framework are more likely to be supported and enhanced with ongoing professional learning. Professional learning accommodates teachers as learners, recognizes the long-term nature of learning, and uses methods that are likely to lead teachers to improve their practice as professionals (Gaible & Burns, 2005, p. 16). Examples of professional learning as it ties into the leadership framework are ongoing workshops (Domain 2c), research (Domain 2a), mentoring and coaching (Domain 2a), peer training (Domain 2c), reflection (Domain 1e), observations (Domain 4a), and infusion of technology (Domain 3d).

Aligning Professional Learning to District and School Goals

Professional learning is not an isolated activity. The learning should be focused on identified areas. It is essential that the professional learning plan be in concert with the district and/or school goals.

Compelling evidence suggests that school leaders are much better served when professional learning is focused on the deep, thoughtful, and consistent implementation of a few things. That is contrary to the general trend of professional learning in educational institutions, which is characterized by the introduction of many new initiatives and ideas but deep implementation of few, if any. Just as fragmented efforts are ineffective at the organizational level, they are equally ineffective for the individual leader (Reeves, 2010, p. 53).

The leadership framework is the starting block for the development of a professional learning plan. After an analysis of the personal reflection and/or evaluative data from the leadership framework, the leader should identify two or three key areas for potential improvement. Identification of areas that demonstrate unsatisfactory or basic levels of performance should be targeted for professional learning.

These identified areas should then be coupled with initiatives or goals currently in place at the district or school level for the leader to develop a professional learning plan that includes not only the goals for their own leadership enhancement but also supports the direction and initiatives of the district and school.

In developing professional learning plan goals, those goals should be:

- *Cyclical.* As learning is ongoing, so are goals. When a goal is attained, the next goal should be easily identified to continue the improvement process.
- *Differentiated.* Identified goals need not be accomplished in the same manner, time frame, or model. A number of leaders may have the same professional learning plan goal, but accomplishing that goal may be collaborative or individual.
- *Monitored.* The improvement process can be effective only if the learner is aware of the expected outcome and the progress made toward attainment. Benchmark monitoring throughout the learning process.
- *Results driven.* All goals should be purposeful and have a specific intended outcome. The positive results are the target for the learning.
- *Embedded.* The professional learning should not be an add-on or extra work but rather embedded in the leader's ongoing daily work.

Planning to Use *The Leadership Framework*

Collins (2001) identifies the *Hedgehog Concept* as a suggestion for disciplined thought: hedgehogs are those who keep looking at the goal and don't get distracted, whereas foxes keep jumping from one thing to another. Hedgehogs make decisions with their most important values and vision in focus. Keeping the eyes, ears, head, and heart focused on learning is not easy, but it may be the most important thing a leader does. To maintain focus on the goals, values, and vision is the ideal path for the hedgehog leader. The use of the leadership framework will guide the professional learning plan concept.

Designing a professional learning plan includes four steps. First, set goals. A goal is a written statement describing where we want to be. Use of a *SMART goal* format is recommended (Roy, 2007). SMART goals include five criteria:

1. *Specific.* Goals must use explicit language. The language used should be aligned with the organization's goals and vision. The goal focuses on high-priority issues.
2. *Measurable.* The goal must include how a change will be calculated. The goal identifies the tools used to measure whether the intended result is achieved.
3. *Attainable.* The goal includes baseline data and the identification of time, resources, and stakeholder ownership for achievement. Can the goal be achieved?
4. *Results oriented.* The goal specifically identifies outcomes that are measurable or observable.
5. *Time bound.* Goals identify the amount of time required to accomplish it. A predetermined time frame can create a sense of urgency and make the goal a priority.

In short, SMART goals assist in determining which of the efforts is making a difference, encourage setting benchmarks to monitor achievement, and identify specific evaluation measures.

The second component in the design of a professional learning plan is to define the *objectives.* What needs to be improved? How is it aligned to the leadership framework and the district/school goals?

Third, the *monitoring system* achieving the goals is critical. How will you know whether the goal has been achieved? How will you know whether it is effective? Identifying benchmarks for monitoring evidence throughout the plan is essential.

Finally, the professional learning plan should include a designated time to review the outcomes. Were the goals appropriate to achieve the intended results? If so, now what? If not, why not? When leaders embark on implementing professional learning goals, a clear vision and the intended outcomes should be well developed. DuFour et al. (2010) suggests the following considerations using professional learning goals to focus on results, which align to *the leadership framework* in the following manner:

- Less is more—Limiting the number of goals reflects the priority of the focused work. (Domain 1a)
- Align all professional learning goals to district and school goals (Domain 2c).
- Use a separate template for each goal. The template should provide the structure to focus on improved results, rather than on just implementing activities (Domain 2c).
- Include ongoing progress monitoring in the learning process. Clarity is necessary in how the achievement of the goal will be attained, monitored, and measured (Domain 2c).
- Celebrate progress (Domain 1e).
- Be wary of complacency that may set in when a goal has been achieved. Learning is an ongoing process (Domain 2b) (pp. 176–177).

Textbox 7.4 summarizes elements of a *professional learning and growth plan*.

Textbox 7.4. Elements of a Professional Learning and Growth Plan

- Active leader and supervisor collaboration
- Research and evidence based
- Driven by measurable goals
- Contains a mutually agreed upon action plan
- Includes a manageable timetable
- Resources are listed and reviewed
- Evidence is collected and analyzed
- Builds leadership knowledge and skills
- Includes best leadership strategies and practices
- Improves teacher and student performance

Summary

The purpose of this chapter was to define and examine models of professional learning. Because learning is a lifelong process, and we all have the ability to learn, many models of professional learning can be successful if properly implemented. It is appropriate to use a variety of models as they align with the purpose of the professional learning and learning style of the learner. Professional learning models should neither be chosen nor evaluated as effective based on a single criterion. Training opportunities are appropriate for learning specified tasks or procedures.

It is critical to align personal professional learning to the goals of the district, school, and individual. The leader can to be more effective when goals are focused, embedded in his daily work, monitored, and results driven. One example of using the leadership framework will serve as the foundation for the design and development of a professional learning and growth plan for leaders, as you will see in chapter 8.

Case Study

You have been hired recently as the principal of Addison Elementary School. During the interview process, you are made aware that, unless things change, the state may place the school on academic probation. Student achievement has been declining significantly over the past five years. The building leadership has been consistently unstable. Teachers are feeling frustrated with the perceived lack of support from the previous building administrators and district office administration. Four school improvement initiatives, (1) literacy and mathematics, (2) one-to-one technology for all students, (3) a districtwide data warehouse, and (4) a revised report card program, have all been implemented within the past three years by previous building and district leaders with no evidence of improvement in student learning.

The superintendent has indicated that, during last year's institute days, only one day of professional growth activities were provided in a large-group setting for each of the four initiatives. In your review of the past sessions, you believe that professional learning and practice were inadequate and ineffective to fully implement the initiatives with fidelity. Your first task as the new principal is to develop strategies to shift Addison Elementary School from poor performance to achieving improved student growth while improving instructional practices. Develop a school-wide professional learning plan that considers the impact of the four initiatives on student learning and provides faculty and staff the necessary professional growth to experience confidence and success.

Discussion Questions

1. Given the four initiatives for the school, how will you prioritize them to achieve the greatest impact for improved student learning?
2. How will you assess the previous professional learning of the faculty?
3. In reviewing the different models for professional learning, which models do you believe will be most effective for the teachers of Addison Elementary School?
4. Design a timetable for professional learning opportunities for the upcoming school year. Identify the target audience, dates, time frame, required resources, costs, and expected outcomes.
5. Develop an assessment or monitoring tool for the professional learning opportunities. How will you know whether the expected outcomes have been achieved? What data will you collect and analyze?
6. Plan a feedback loop for the participants of the professional learning. What personal reflections, data, and evidence are needed to best evaluate the impact of the new learning?
7. What evidence will you collect in the classrooms to ensure that the implementation of new learning to support student achievement is occurring?

Self-Assessment and Reflection

Reflect on your own professional goals, learning style, time constraints, and resources. Which models of professional learning would you most likely choose? Give examples of professional learning that you have personally found effective and those that have been least effective. To what do you attribute the difference?

References

Carter, M. (2015). Supervising or coaching—What's the difference? Retrieved from http://www.cocoaches.net/uploads/Supervising-or-coaching.pdf

Collins, J. (2001). *Good to great: Why some companies make the leap . . . and others don't.* New York, NY: HarperCollins.

Darling-Hammond, L., Chung Weir, R., Andree, A., & Richardson, N. (2009). *Professional learning in the learning profession: A status report on teacher development in the United States and abroad.* Oxford, OH: National Staff Development Council.

DuFour, R. (1991). *The principal as staff developer.* Bloomington, IN: National Educational Service.

DuFour, R., DuFour, R., Eaker, R., & Many, T. (2010). *Learning by doing: A handbook for professional learning communities at work.* (2nd ed.). Bloomington, IN: Solution Tree Press.

DuFour, R., & Eaker, R. (1998). *Professional learning communities at work.* Bloomington, IN: Solution Tree.

DuFour, R., Eaker, R., & DuFour, R. (2005). *On common ground: The power of professional learning communities.* Bloomington, IN: Solution Tree.

Gaible, E., & Burns, M. (2005). *Using technology to train teachers: Appropriate uses of ICT for teacher professional development in developing countries.* Washington, DC: Dev/World Bank.

Joyce, B., & Showers, B. (1995). *Student development through staff development.* (2nd ed.). White Plains, NY: Longman.

Kaser, J., Mundry, S., Stiles, K., & Loucks-Horsley, S. (2006). *Leading every day: 124 actions for effective leadership.* Thousand Oaks, CA: Sage.

Learning Forward. (2011). *Standards for professional learning.* Oxford, OH: Author.

Management Mentors. (2013). *Coaching vs. mentoring: 25 ways they're different.* Retrieved from http://www.slideshare.net/oleksandrkonytskyy/coaching-vs-mentoring-25-ways-theyre-different

Psencik, K. (2011). *The coach's craft: Powerful practices to support school leaders.* Oxford, OH: Learning Forward.

Reeves, D. B. (2010). *Transforming professional development into student results.* Alexandria, VA: Association of Supervision and Curriculum Development.

Roy, P. (2007). *A toolkit for quality professional development in Arkansas.* Oxford, OH: NSCD.

Shorter Oxford English Dictionary. (2002). (5th ed.). New York, NY: Oxford University Press.

Solution Tree. (2007). *Professional learning communities: An overview.* Bloomington, IN: Author.

Walker, T. (2013, April 29). *No more sit and get: Rebooting teacher professional development.* Washington, DC: National Education Association.

~

CHAPTER EIGHT

Using *The Leadership Framework* in Supervision and Evaluation

Supervision can be the linchpin for deep school improvement.

—Sergiovanni and Starratt

Objectives

At the conclusion of this chapter you will be able to:

1. Relate the importance of professional learning and growth as major influences in improving leader effectiveness (PSEL 1, 2, 3, 6, 8, 10; NELP 1, 2, 3, 4, 5, 6, 7).
2. Distinguish the different yet interrelated processes between evaluation and supervision (PSEL 1, 2, 3, 4, 6, 9, 10; NELP 1, 2, 3, 7).
3. Explain the relationship between supervision and professional learning and growth (PSEL 1, 2, 3, 4, 6, 9, 10; NELP 1, 2, 3, 7).
4. Explain the relationship between evaluation and professional learning and growth (PSEL 1, 2, 3, 4, 6, 9, 10; NELP 1, 2, 3, 7).
5. Designate the functions of *The Leadership Framework* in supervision and evaluation (PSEL 1, 2, 3, 4, 5, 6, 7, 8, 9, 10; NELP 1, 2, 3, 4, 5, 6, 7).

Professional Growth

The professional and personal needs of the novice leader are far different from those of an experienced leader; however, we hold these leaders to the same expectations of competency and professionalism. The question becomes how to differentiate supervision and evaluation of these leaders and how to help them grow in their leadership knowledge and skills. All leaders have different needs as they examine their own professional learning and growth.

Novice leaders need more intensive support and more frequent feedback to grow into highly effective practitioners than many district evaluation systems are designed to provide. The reality is that even the best-prepared leaders need time and assistance to apply their knowledge and skills to their individual schools and districts. If supervision and evaluation are truly the focal point of a performance management and professional growth system, they must be paired with structured support and ongoing, data-driven feedback that a comprehensive performance program should provide.

Too often, professional development activities are structured as a one size fits all. Most school districts use only a small portion of their budget for professional learning and growth activities for school or district leaders. Most often, no specific professional growth program is planned for these leaders. They are usually combined with the same professional development given to the teaching or the support staff. And often, neither the leaders nor the support staff is even included in professional growth opportunities.

Those activities leaders do attend may be relevant, but they often overlook the requirements needed for an effective leader. It appears that school districts are not investing in the most important part of personnel management—ongoing, sustained learning and growth for those important leaders, a valued human resource supporting the district schools.

Yet leaders use professional growth and learning activities in planning continuous opportunities for teachers to grow in pedagogical techniques, knowledge, and content skills. This type of growth is often teacher driven and geared directly to the individual needs of that teacher. These activities usually appear in the individual teacher supervision and evaluation plan.

But what about those activities needed for the leader to grow in leadership knowledge and skills? Where do these fit into an individual leader supervision and professional evaluation plan? This is where *The Leadership Framework* can provide a tool for dialogue, direction, and structure in a comprehensive and relevant professional growth plan for a leader. Chapter 7 outlined the uses of a professional learning and growth plan. Refer back to textbox 7.4, which provided the elements of an effective and ongoing professional learning and growth plan.

Previous chapters have illustrated how *The Leadership Framework* provides a relevant model of knowledge, skills, dispositions, and practices for effective leadership. This model can be incorporated into an effective plan for goal development, assessment of those goals, and the supervision and evaluation in implementation of those goals.

As best practice strategies for leadership continue to emerge in the literature, the standards-based movement and the licensing of educators have helped to develop recommendations for leadership preparation programs and the evaluation of leaders. The early history of leadership development includes few suggested formal processes for evaluation of effective leadership.

Goal setting was based on simple tasks. Leaders were evaluated on the effectiveness of management skills, such as orderly hallways, a clean school, providing adequate supplies for the classrooms and programs, and discipline handled with fair and efficient strategies. Yet in the past several decades, the functions required of leaders have become much more complex. The literature calls for the leader to be an effective instructional leader with expert management and people skills, assessment knowledge, and skilled fiscal resource management.

Supervision and Building the Capacity for Growth

Educational research has repeatedly identified effective teaching and leadership as critical factors in student learning. The work that leaders accomplish in schools and classrooms matters, so one of a district's ongoing top priorities should be to find, hire, and develop leaders.

Supervision is formative: It provides coaching and mentoring to build leadership capacity and helps guide novice and experienced leaders in searching out best research for sustained personal growth. Evaluation is summative: It generally is described as having two primary purposes—first, measuring performance and, second, providing individualized feedback and support to strengthen professional performance.

Many leadership supervision and evaluation procedures school districts adopt do little to affect performance. Typically, leaders view the supervision and evaluation procedures as bureaucratic hurdles that must be cleared. They are simply one more task leaders must accomplish. This roadblock is magnified by the fact that many administrative supervision and evaluation plans do not require supervisors to visit schools or to review specific leadership actions in an ongoing manner to promote accountability and growth.

It is appropriate to discuss how to supervise and evaluate leaders effectively so the process is relevant to them and improves their leadership practice. Leadership supervision and evaluation must be guided by two major points: First, effective school leadership is central to effective teacher supervision and evaluation, and, second, just as teacher supervision and evaluation should be comprehensive, so should leadership supervision and evaluation.

District leaders are essential to ensure meaningful school leadership supervision and evaluation. District leadership must adopt comprehensive and fair supervision and evaluation policies and practices. Most importantly, district leaders must hold school leaders accountable to be in teacher classrooms daily and weekly. This includes the central belief that district leaders are responsible to train and monitor evaluators in how to ensure that teachers are providing high-quality instruction.

Effective supervisors routinely visit schools and provide formative, relevant, and appropriate feedback to leaders. Visiting schools on a routine basis is critical. How can we create a clear picture of leader effectiveness unless we formally and informally visit schools and classrooms multiple times per year? If we expect school leaders to be in all teacher classrooms weekly, for extended periods of time, then district leaders must hold them accountable for performing this task. If leader development and personal growth is a priority, then district leaders must find a way to visit schools and teacher classrooms routinely. Districts must define effective leadership and be clear about how to measure it.

The recent trend of using standardized or high stakes state testing data as the standard for school effectiveness is flawed. Teaching is a social endeavor having many complex variables affecting student learning, and leaders are significant in those variables. Student test scores should be used as one piece of data in a comprehensive leadership supervision and evaluation model. However, equally important is data collected from such varied sources as:

- classroom observations (assessed by principals, teacher leaders, instructional coaches, or peers);
- student assessment data on various indicators focused on growth (mostly formative assessments);
- instructional artifacts, such as student work, scoring rubrics, and lesson plans;
- teacher self-reflection in journals or logs;
- age-appropriate student or parent surveys; and
- teacher-developed professional development/growth plans.

One key factor in selecting data sources is to ensure that leaders have buy-in about what they perceive as fair and representative of their leadership performance. But supervisors should also have nonnegotiables in the process. These nonnegotiables may include:

- relevant and age-appropriate instructional schedules,
- clearly identified and posted essential learning standards in "student-friendly" language,
- a school-wide behavior plan that supports and aligns with the district and school vision and mission, and
- ongoing opportunities for students to achieve subject matter mastery.

The school and district environment in which the leaders work may determine other nonnegotiables. Supervisors must solicit feedback about leadership performance expectations throughout the supervisory process if they expect the procedures to affect day-to-day school-wide classroom instructional practice (Tomal et al., 2015).

When district leaders wear the supervisory hat, they are coaching, mentoring, collaborating, and actively assisting leaders in the school setting. They become another set of eyes and ears in the school and classrooms helping to monitor and improve student learning. The district leader creates opportunities for collaborative dialogue with the school leader to discuss classroom management systems, student behavior programs, instructional methodology, current research, and student learning goals.

The supervisory hat permits the district leader to be a mentor and to guide the school leader to relevant and effective research in best practices. Together the district leader and school leader can develop relevant goals for growth that directly affect the day-to-day learning of students, teachers, and support staff. Textbox 8.1 lists the elements of an effective and ongoing supervisory process.

Textbox 8.1.   Qualities of an Effective Supervision Plan

- Mutual collaboration and sharing of ideas
- Measurable and relevant goals
- Active coaching and mentoring
- Relevant constructive feedback
- Multiple site visits (informal and formal)
- Active monitoring by supervisor
- Conflict mediation when needed
- Monitors, records, and analyzes outcomes

Generally speaking, all leaders can benefit from good coaching and mentoring. Mentoring can help leaders in dealing with disruptive students, personal problems that affect teaching, administrative requirements, state and district reporting, and clarifying the responsibilities of the position. District leaders should be well trained in how to be effective supervisors in the mentoring and coaching process.

In supervision, the relationship between supervisor and school leader is critical to success in personal and professional growth. Topics for coaching and mentoring may include understanding instruction and curriculum, managing student discipline, understanding the school district operations, and district policies and procedures. In addition to these professional qualities, a mentor needs effective coaching skills, including being personal, sensitive, and understanding and establishing rapport and giving constructive feedback (Tomal, Schilling, & Wilhite, 2014).

Finally, note that the summative evaluation process is simply an analysis of data collected during the supervision process. Sustained supervision is the only way to improve leadership practice. Resources need to be devoted to the improvement of these practices rather than simply assigning a rating to performance. What, then, is the necessary role of evaluation in the supervision and evaluation process?

Evaluation and Building Capacity for Growth

Like students, leaders are learners. The best way to improve student learning is to strengthen the instructional practices of leaders through job-embedded professional learning opportunities. Evaluation systems play a critical role in informing this work, and the ones conceived with this in mind will be most likely to succeed.

Leadership evaluation must focus more on the act of being a leader. Policies and procedures must not only measure performance but also provide pathways to develop and improve practice. A well-designed evaluation plan might better be termed a performance management plan. Its primary purposes must be to maximize the act of leadership and to improve performance. It does so as a critical component of an aligned district-wide process that provides embedded opportunities for leaders to learn and grow continuously.

Evaluation is most effective when it is integrated with other processes that support professional learning and growth. It needs to provide individual leaders with the opportunity to analyze the process, to determine the impact on their individual roles, and to make modifications based on that analysis.

What leaders need is fewer performance ratings and more data-driven feedback on their practice. A commitment to leader ongoing learning, including the creation of personalized professional learning plans, should be a central focus in a comprehensive evaluation process.

These plans should point leaders toward specific and highly relevant learning opportunities that allow them to address areas of leadership that need improvement. It means that evaluators must understand effective leadership. This will happen only when those responsible for evaluating, coaching, and mentoring leaders are trained in the art of providing meaningful, developmental feedback; encouraging reflection; and creating opportunities for professional learning and growth.

If designed as part of a comprehensive plan, feedback on instruction, reflection, and mentoring activities changes professional development from a one-time or infrequent event to continuous growth activities. It is critical that districts build these principles and structures into their evaluation processes because a systemic evaluation plan will succeed or fail based on its ability to improve leadership capacity; instructional pedagogy; and, ultimately, student learning.

Textbox 8.2 lists the elements of an effective evaluation process.

Textbox 8.2. Qualities of an Effective Evaluation Plan

- Research and outcome based
- Relevant and measurable goals
- Developmental and meaningful feedback
- Active reflection
- Opportunities for continuing growth
- Builds leadership knowledge and competencies
- Directly affects teacher and student performance
- Provides a rating of performance

The models or frameworks used for evaluation of leaders must be research based. It is important that the evaluators and the leaders agree upon the model and the process that will be used, have a shared language, and have a common understanding and definition of the elements of effective leadership.

A meaningful evaluation process transitions directly from a relevant supervisory process. An honest evaluation with reliable and constructive feedback based on unbiased evidence will enable leaders to continue to learn and grow. Both are based on developing a collaborative and trusting coaching/mentoring relationship between the leader and the evaluator.

When district leaders wear the evaluator's hat, they gather evidence and data from multiple sources and make judgments about performance. These sources may include student surveys, classroom observations, classroom drop-ins, and student achievement results gleaned from standardized summative and formative district and grade-level assessments. Leaders and the evaluator must analyze all of the data gathered to identify professional growth needs. One comprehensive way to conduct this analysis is through *The Leadership Framework*.

The Leadership Framework, as previously outlined in chapters 1, 2, and 3, divides effective leadership into four domains: Domain 1: Leadership Competencies, Domain 2: Professional Learning and Growth Practices, Domain 3: Instructional Practices, and Domain 4: Management Competencies. *The Leadership Framework* domains have 18 components and 90 elements. *The Leadership Framework* allows leaders to be rated at four performance levels: unsatisfactory, basic, proficient, and distinguished. Such tools and rubrics found in *The Leadership Framework* can help to measure leadership effectiveness successfully and provide leaders with relevant feedback on the factors that matter for improving performance and enhancing professional growth.

School districts can create alignment between evaluator priorities and coaching priorities by using *The Leadership Framework* to guide individual leader evaluation, self-assessment, and mentoring. This necessitates open communication and trust between leaders and evaluators, a shared protocol (common language) for assessing leadership, and a genuine understanding of the culture and climate of the district and schools.

Research-Based Supervision and Evaluation

By enhancing and building on a modified clinical supervision model, we can use *The Leadership Framework* as a tool for change and growth that results in more effective leadership and increased individual growth. The traditional administrative evaluation process has usually followed a one-way progression. This process has typically consisted of the following steps:

- Written notification of a conference—Leader receives a fall notice that an evaluation is due, usually in the spring of the school year. The leader is invited to a conference with the superintendent or a designee to discuss goals and strategies for that school year.
- Conference—Conversation with leader regarding submission of goals, updates, and key dates for submission of information to evaluator. Brief

discussions about management, budgeting, and personnel usually dominate the conference.

- Follow-up conference—Administrator shows up at appointed time and submits a summative narrative of the actions and results from the goal conference earlier in the school year.
- Narrative write-up—Evaluator fills out required district forms for administrative evaluation and provides copies for the administrator according to the required approved time line (which either conforms to state statutes and/or board administrative policy and procedures).
- Post-narrative conference—Leader and evaluator discuss written evaluation and performance rating. Both leader and evaluator sign off as having read and discussed the written document regarding the evaluation process.
- Sign off with signatures—Both parties agree that they have concluded the process required.

Unfortunately, on-site observations rarely or never occur in this model. The effectiveness of the leader may not be representative of what students, teachers, and parents experience on a daily basis.

Often, school districts lack alignment between observation and gathering hard data as evidence. The evaluation cycle includes little or no planning for professional learning and growth for the leader. Basically, the traditional evaluation process is a time-intensive process without much impact on leader effectiveness or teacher–student performance. Leaders become passive recipients in the evaluation process, isolated from their peers. For leaders to grow professionally in an effective evaluation process, they must be active and reflective participants.

When a research-based model is implemented, evaluators and leaders need a training period. They must become familiar with the steps in the supervisory and evaluation process. They must share knowledge and develop a common language defining effective teaching. They must develop a shared understanding of what constitutes effective instruction and the expectations of leaders in that district to meet those expectations.

It is possible that leaders who previously received high performance ratings may now receive lower ratings. This may create an uncomfortable climate for leaders who received high ratings using a traditional supervision and evaluation model based on written narratives every year. In the worst-case scenario, the leader gets neither written feedback nor performance evaluation on a yearly basis.

District leaders need to develop strategies for supporting and improving school leaders throughout the evaluation process. Expectations must be raised. Resources and key learning opportunities are the keys to improving leadership performance when using a research-based evaluation plan. What is important to the evaluation and supervision of leaders is the central premise that leaders must grow in expertise to become more effective in their demanding and complex roles.

The effective district leader should establish clear and fair guidelines for the evaluation supervisory process. These may include:

- the use of a collaborative goal-setting process;
- the establishment of mutually agreed upon nonnegotiables for student achievement and assessment;
- a clear alignment to school improvement plans and the values, vision, mission, and goals of the district and the school;
- a research-based data collection process that monitors and documents ongoing achievement and instructional goals; and
- the allocation of resources to support the goals for achievement and instruction in the school and district.

All of these actions must be implemented collaboratively when working with individual leaders. Guiding this process must be a clear vision and mission for the district and schools supporting the principle that every child can learn. Student performance goals should permit students multiple opportunities to demonstrate what they have learned and that they can use the knowledge and skills identified within the established district curriculum. Creative leadership is central to supporting a systemic use of the professional learning and growth supervisory evaluation process.

Individual Professional Learning and Growth Plans

The use of *The Leadership Framework*, which reflects the National Leadership Preparation Standards, 2018 (NELP) and the Professional Standards for Educational Leaders, 2015 (PSEL), may be one step toward beginning an effective supervision and evaluation plan for leaders.

These standards explicitly demonstrate the purpose of professional learning for educators: to develop the knowledge, skills, practices, and dispositions they need to help students perform at higher levels. The standards are not a prescription for how education leaders and public officials should address all of the challenges related to improving the performance of educators and their students. Instead, they focus on the central issue of professional traits and competencies evident in successful and effective leaders.

So, if an evaluator creates the environment for effective evaluation, the dialogue between the evaluator and leader would include a discussion of those domains in *The Leadership Framework* combined with what constitutes effective leadership as demonstrated in standards such as NELP, 2018, and PSEL, 2015. These, then, become the foundation on which to build the supervisory and evaluation process.

To develop a new perspective for leader-focused professional learning and growth, it is necessary to create a learning organization with identified leadership learning communities committed to continuous improvement, collective accountability, and goal alignment. Allotting time and resources for this leadership community to collaborate on a regular basis during the school day, months, and year is a requirement.

In addition, training in teaming skills will help transform the culture and climate for the individual, group, and the organization. If smaller districts cannot accommodate this type of learning community within the district, it may be necessary to join with surrounding smaller districts into a larger, more relevant leadership community. The point is this: Leaders need support, which is best accomplished in collaboration with others in the same or similar roles. Supervisors and evaluators must act as instructional leaders. They must articulate the overall vision and mission of the district.

The overarching principle is that all students must have the opportunity to master the knowledge and skills identified in an articulated curriculum aligned with national and state standards. Finally, fundamentally, leaders, teachers, and students need to be lifelong learners with continuous individual, group, and organizational improvement as the underlying foundation of the district as a learning community.

Even though each leader is looked upon as a lifelong learner in a professional learning community, it is important to differentiate the need for and the quantity of supervision and evaluation of the leaders. Leaders who receive performance ratings such as distinguished, exceeding, or excellent, depending on the rating scale used, may not need to be evaluated every year. Leaders who receive performance ratings such as proficient or satisfactory may need to be evaluated every other year and encouraged to enhance their personal and professional growth.

However, novice leaders who need much coaching and mentoring, and those experienced leaders who receive ratings such as basic, unsatisfactory, or needs improvement must be monitored more closely on an annual basis. If their status remains unchanged, consideration should be given to dismissal because they may not have the ability to grow or improve or they are choosing not to. Addressing the unsatisfactory and marginal leader is necessary in an effective district supervisory and evaluation plan. Schools cannot continue to grow and function with ineffective and poorly functioning leadership; they consistently become labeled for watch lists or in need of improvement. Most importantly, the performance level of the children in these schools is compromised, and learning may be delayed.

Ineffective school leaders affect student performance in a profoundly negative way. It is unfair to the students attending an ineffective or marginal school because they may not have the same opportunities to perform as their peers who are enrolled in a more effective school. Field research has clearly documented that effective classroom practices in higher-performing schools result in higher-achieving learners.

Mid-continent Research for Education and Learning (McREL) conducted a study on what works in a large-scale, systematic way. Their meta-analysis reviewed decades of studies focused on teacher classroom practice; then, they selected the most rigorous from an initial sampling of 4,000 such studies. McREL's researchers mathematically determined the most effective practices found to have a statistically significant impact on student learning measured by standardized test scores.

First published in 2001, this study described in *Classroom Instruction That Works* (Marzano, Pickering, & Pollock, 2001) changed teaching by linking classroom strategies to evidence of increased student learning. The work clearly identifies successful approaches that mark effective classroom instruction. The basic premise of the study shows that schools that use research to guide instructional practices outperform those that do not.

In a companion book, *What Works in Schools*, Marzano (2003) describes 11 research-based factors shown in another large-scale research project at McREL to be essential for the larger context of an effective school. The study is a follow-up to that done in 2001 and verifies once again that teacher effectiveness is of high importance. The study is divided into three areas: school, teacher, and student factors.

The school factors are a guaranteed and viable curriculum, challenging goals and effective feedback, parent and community involvement, a safe and orderly environment, and collegiality and professionalism. The teacher factors are instructional strategies, classroom management, and effective curriculum design. The student factors are home environment, learned intelligence and background knowledge, and motivation. These 11 factors lead to the conclusion that school effectiveness and teacher effectiveness are highly interrelated in how a student learns (Marzano, 2003).

In his 90-90-90 studies (more than 90 percent poverty, more than 90 percent minorities, more than 90 percent achieving at high proficiency levels), Reeves (2005) shows that high-poverty schools can also be high performing. He provides examples from multiple school systems to illustrate the common characteristics of 90-90-90 schools. The examples identified these factors: a strong focus on academic achievement, clear curriculum choices, frequent assessment of student progress and multiple opportunities for improvement, an emphasis on nonfiction writing, and collaborative scoring of student work, with explicit guidelines.

Reeves stresses that teacher quality and effective leadership, not demographics, are the most dominant factors in determining student success. The effective practices and policies identified in those studies are entirely consistent with the McREL findings. Effective leaders can use these types of studies to improve the teaching and learning in schools and guide ongoing and effective professional learning opportunities. Relevant professional learning and tracking individual teacher growth are vital to creating effective teachers.

That is why professional and learning growth plans are essential for effective leaders, who evaluate and supervise teachers. That is one of the reasons why evaluators of leaders need to have the moral courage to deal with unsatisfactory and marginal leaders. It is an unpleasant task, but it is an ethical task that needs to be carried through if we are following a vision of an organization, all of whose members are lifelong learners. True instructional leaders ensure that every child receives an equal opportunity to learn with an effective teacher and an equally effective leader.

In this environment, leaders are expected to continue to learn, to improve, and to become more effective in their roles. The expectations are set by the norms of the learning organization and its collective members. This has a profound impact on the entire district and schools as each leader becomes more effective, no matter his performance level. It is possible that a whole professional learning organization collectively and individually demonstrates improvement. This improvement positively affects the learning goals and performance levels of the students the organization serves.

In the research-based environment, accountability and more supervisory hands-on guidance and coaching are required. As an instructional leader, the school and district leaders are in classrooms a majority of their time. In addition, effective leaders use the talent and expertise of identified effective teacher leaders to coach and mentor those peers who are given an unsatisfactory or needs improvement rating to help improve teacher effectiveness.

District leaders who are planning for school leader growth must develop capacity and advocate and create support systems for professional learning.

They must prioritize, monitor, and coordinate resources and make them available for each leader, no matter his level of experience. Multiple forms and sources of data should be used to identify individual needs as the evaluator plans, assesses, and evaluates professional leadership knowledge, skills, and traits (see Textbox 7.4).

Using this model for professional learning and growth, we can begin an effective and comprehensive goal-setting evaluation process. Appendix B contains several sample plans for professional learning and growth. They are outlined for easy understanding using *The Leadership Framework*, which fits well into an overall process for supervision and evaluation.

Each sample plan is aligned to *The Leadership Framework* with a component aligned to a goal or goals set by the leader. The evaluator and the leader being evaluated could prepare two to three goals aligned to one or more of the four domains for the performance supervision and evaluation process. The chosen domain components can be easily aligned to the PSEL or NELP standards demonstrating leadership effectiveness.

Each goal has an established time line, person responsible, action steps, and evidence of what was accomplished within the time frame established. Using such a tool to supervise and evaluate a school or district leader allows for the fair and transparent process of performance rating and, more importantly, sustained professional growth the leader controls while benefiting the school and district stakeholders.

The application of a research-based approach to supervision and evaluation should be applied with sustained support during implementation until long-term change is embedded in the organization's culture. The evaluation process should be an outgrowth of the supervisory process. The outcomes should align with national and state standards, content standards, district vision and mission, school improvement plans, and, most importantly, the expected learning goals of the district. The ultimate goals must always be improved student performance paired with leader and teacher continuing professional growth.

Summary

An analysis of research data indicates that effective leadership is one of the most important variables directly affecting student performance. All children deserve to have an effective leader in their school. Research and field practice have defined what elements comprise relevant and effective professional development plans. Such district and school plans must contain multiple learning and growth opportunities. These activities must target individual professional learning and growth based on the needs of the leader and his level of experience and background in a leadership role. *The Leadership Framework* can become an active and useful tool in professional and learning plans.

How do we support and encourage leaders to become more effective in what they do? By using a research-based and comprehensive evaluation and supervision plan focused on individual needs. This requires district leaders to act as effective evaluators and supervisors. They must be in schools and classrooms on a regular basis, provide immediate and reliable feedback about what was observed, and provide constructive suggestions for growth.

At the same time, an improved formal evaluation process must emerge that requires school and district leaders to use information gathered from multiple sources, such as walk-throughs, student surveys, and other methods of gathering data over time. This enhanced process allows the evaluator to become more informed about the leader's performance as well as the climate and culture of the school and the classrooms.

Effective supervision and evaluation must reflect a true picture of the daily life of a leader, the students, and the teachers in that school. Using all of the data collected, the leader and evaluator can identify professional needs and develop an individual professional learning and growth plan with goals, action steps, time line, person responsible, resources, and evidence of completion. All leaders will have a professional learning and growth plan. Everyone will be considered a lifelong learner and an active participant in the professional learning community with a goal of becoming a more effective and skilled leader.

Case Study

You have been appointed the new principal of Madison Middle School. In your induction with the superintendent, you extensively discussed supervision and evaluation of faculty. Your district recently added professional learning and growth plans to the collective bargaining agreement's approved supervision and evaluation process, which includes final performance ratings of excellent, proficient, basic, and unsatisfactory. Your superintendent brought to your attention that this plan applies to all school and district leaders. The district uses *The Leadership Framework* as part of the supervision and evaluation process for school and district leaders. You know that, as a novice leader, you have much to learn.

Your superintendent has scheduled a conference for you to decide jointly the focus elements in Domains 3 and 4 of *The Leadership Framework* for your first year as principal. Review these components before you attend the conference with your superintendent. Think about what you will suggest to her about your professional and personal growth. What areas do you wish to focus on in your first year? What types of support do you think you will need?

Discussion Questions

1. What two to three elements of Domains 3 and 4 will you focus your attention on in your first year as a new principal?
2. What will your professional learning plan list as possible activities for consideration as evidence of your performance in these elements?
3. What steps will you take to collect appropriate data to support your actions?
4. What evidence will you determine is needed so you receive a fair and accurate appraisal of your performance?
5. What steps will you take to establish a positive relationship with your superintendent?
6. What is the difference between evaluation and supervision? Can an evaluator wear both hats at the same time? If so, how?
7. Why is it important for a district to select a framework for supervision and evaluation that all leaders can use? How does this framework help leaders become more effective?

Self-Assessment and Reflection

Develop a professional learning and growth plan for yourself based on your identified needs and professional goals. Using the leadership framework, develop a plan that includes the following: domains, measurable goals, action steps, time line, resources, person responsible, evidence submitted, and what impact and application it has on your role as a school or a district leader. What kind of professional development would you suggest to leaders so that they would become familiar with the leadership framework?

References

Marzano, R. (2003). *What works in schools: Translating research into action.* Alexandria, VA: Association for Supervision and Curriculum Development.

Marzano, R., Pickering, D., & Pollock, J. (2001). *Classroom instruction that works: Research-based strategies for increasing student achievement.* Alexandria, VA: Association for Supervision and Curriculum Development.

Reeves, D. (2005). *Accountability in action: A blueprint for learning organizations*. (2nd ed.). Denver, CO: Advanced Learning Press.

Sergiovanni, T. and Starratt, R. (2006). *Supervision: A redefinition*. London, England: McGraw-Hill Education-Europe.

Tomal, D., Schilling, C., & Wilhite, R. (2014). *The teacher leader: Core competencies and strategies for effective leadership*. Lanham, MD: Rowman & Littlefield Education, Inc.

Tomal, D., Wilhite, R., Phillips, B., Sims, P., & Gibson, N. (2015). *Supervision and evaluation for learning and growth*. Lanham, MD: Rowman & Littlefield Education, Inc.

~

The Framework for Effective Leadership

Domain 1: *Leadership Competencies*

1a. Establishes a solid foundation
- develops and upholds the mission, vision, values, and goals of the school
- identifies benchmarks, expectations, and feedback measures to ensure accountability
- acts as a decision maker
- serves as a change agent
- builds caring effective relationships with stakeholders
- practices accessible, approachable, and engaged role in school
- epitomizes resilience

1b. Builds shared leadership
- advocates for staff and students
- works collaboratively with stakeholders
- promotes development of teacher/administrative leaders
- delegates tasks based on interests and skill sets
- builds consensus with appropriate stakeholders
- supports innovative thinking and risk-taking efforts

1c. Initiates effective communication
- uses verbal, nonverbal, and written means effectively
- articulates programs, progress, and needs
- recognizes and celebrates accomplishments of students and staff
- facilitates professional dialogue

- promotes identification, analysis, and use of creative solutions to problems
- considers all opinions in a respectful and open manner
- elicits others' opinions in decision making

1d. Adheres to a moral compass
- models integrity, fairness, honesty, and respect
- maintains professional dispositions
- works for educational and not personal gain
- demonstrates the application of ethics and justice
- models and applies an understanding of the cultural context of the community
- encourages and inspires others to higher levels of commitment, performance, and motivation

1e. Promotes a positive school culture
- establishes an environment of trust, tolerance, respect, and rapport
- advocates equity, fairness, and diversity
- sustains a safe and educationally sound climate
- responds to needs of stakeholders
- demonstrates cultural responsiveness
- encourages inquiry and reflection

Domain 2: *Professional Learning and Growth Practices*
2a. Demonstrates competence as an educational leader
- researches new educational concepts and effectively incorporates ideas in the district
- participates actively in professional learning
- provides mentoring and coaching opportunities
- models accountability/responsibility
- differentiates interactions with boards and organizations

2b. Fosters and facilitates continual improvement
- identifies areas of discourse
- identifies target areas and evaluates strategies for growth
- monitors progress of instruction and evaluates student learning
- evaluates programs and processes on a regular basis

2c. Promotes professional learning and growth
- ensures appropriate timing, time frame, and fiscal commitment
- provides opportunities for professional learning both in and out of district
- uses gifts and talents of district/school staff to peer train
- aligns to individual and school/district goals

- ensures that participants articulate, document, and reflect upon goals
- encourages collaborative, ongoing work resulting in positive change
- models lifelong learning and skill acquisition

2d. Supports school personnel
- demonstrates understanding of content and various instructional strategies
- provides follow-through with discipline referrals in accordance with district/school policies
- protects instructional time
- fosters climate that supports high expectations
- provides resources, time, roles, and structure imperative to sound instruction

Domain 3: *Instructional Practices*

3a. Champions and supports curriculum development
- develops, implements, and revises curriculum
- monitors indicators of student success
- demands equity and accessibility to curriculum and resources
- refines use of multiple resources for effectiveness
- focuses on quality over quantity

3b. Advocates for instruction that supports the needs of all learners
- provides teachers with data to drive instruction and the training to execute
- calls for evidence of alignment between curriculum, instruction, assessment, and professional learning
- promotes differentiated instruction
- recognizes students as active learners
- supports instruction that is engaging, rigorous, and relevant
- encourages student choice and ownership of one's educational pathways

3c. Analyzes assessments
- reflects on and compliments instructional practices
- uses assessment data in ways appropriate to their intended use
- explores gaps in expectations and opportunities to improve
- uses multiple measures of student learning and relevant quality indicators

3d. Incorporates technology to enhance learning
- provides the professional learning/training
- dedicates fiscal resources for the upgrade, purchase, and ongoing training needed
- expects integration of technology for a 21st-century education

- oversees programs and licensure compliance
- commits to timely technology support

Domain 4: *Management Competencies*

4a. Adheres to personnel requirements
- recruits, trains, supports, and retains highly competent personnel
- understands and participates in conflict management
- demands fidelity to the evaluation process in accordance with roles
- supervises subordinates applicably

4b. Reports accurately and in a timely manner
- establishes metrics, collects and analyzes data, interprets and articulates results
- complies with local, state, and federal reporting
- explains and reports to stakeholders in language they can understand

4c. Upholds rules and regulations
- upholds federal, state, and local laws, policies, and regulations
- applies understanding of district policy, privacy, security, acceptable use, and online safety
- applies understanding of copyrights and intellectual property
- manages legal and contractual agreements
- creates and maintains records
- demonstrates knowledge of collective bargaining

4d. Practices and refines resourcefulness
- establishes partnerships
- investigates creative funding opportunities
- uses outside resources
- aligns and evaluates fiscal, human, and material resources

4e. Manages effectively
- prioritizes time with regard to projects
- oversees systems and processes
- oversees scheduling and maintenance of facility
- balances personal and professional responsibilities

APPENDIX B

~

Sample Professional Learning and Growth Plans

Sample plan for superintendents is shown in table B.1. Sample plan for principals is shown in table B.2. Sample plan for other district-level administrators is shown in table B.3. And, finally, a sample plan for assistant principals/teacher leaders or other school leaders is shown in table B.4.

Table B.1. Sample Professional Learning and Growth Plan for Superintendent

Date: _____

District: _____

Name: _____

Position: Superintendent

Evaluator: Board committee or entire board

Performance Rating: _____

Domain 3: Instructional Practices
PSEL, 2015, standards 1, 4, 6, 10
NELP, 2018, standards 1, 4, 6, 7
Goal: Increase student growth by x percent in identified student populations across district schools.

Action Steps	Time	Resources	Person	Evidence
A. Identify district student performance goals and indicators to measure them for the district, each school, and each student subgroup.	2019–2020 school year	Allocate budget for stipends to pay district leadership team for work over the summer.	Superintendent and members, board of education	1. Student performance data reported at August board meeting
1. Analyze student test data and determine goals for the district, each school, and each student subgroup.				2. Student performance learning goals, curriculum plans, instructional resources presented at subseqent board meeting
2. Select indicators that will measure student performance in the district, at each school, and for each subgroup.		Conduct planning and research meetings to review and evaluate findings.		
B. Identify research-based instructional strategies.				
1. Direct assistant superintendent/principals to identify research-based instructional strategies to be used by all teachers in classrooms.				
2. Direct assistant superintendent/principals to develop a professional learning and growth plan for teachers.				

Table B.2. Sample Professional Learning and Growth Plan for Principal

Date: _____
District: _____
School: _____

Name: _____
Position: Principal
Evaluator: Superintendent or designee

Performance Rating:

Domain 2: Professional Learning and Growth Practices
PSEL, 2015, standards 1, 4, 6, 10
NELP, 2018, standards 1, 4, 6, 7
Goal: Increase student growth;
expand teacher instructional strategies.

Action Steps	Time	Resources	Person	Evidence
A. Develop a School Leadership Team.	2019–2020 school year	Allocate funds to pay district school leaders & team members for work over the summer.	Principal	1. Student performance data from last school year reported at August board meeting.
1. Select teacher leaders who are representative of school stakeholders to serve on the school leadership team.				
2. Examine indicator data to identify school faculty needs for learning and growth.				2. Student performance goals for new school year presented at August board meeting.
3. Facilitate preparation of the school professional learning and growth plan for faculty and staff.	2019–2020 school year	Money for release time for school leaders & team to meet, train, and coach and mentor teachers during the school day.		3. School professional learning and growth plan.
B. Create organizational processes and procedures that will develop a culture that values continuous improvement and lifelong learning.				4. Interdisciplinary team agendas, minutes, recommendations for next meeting.
1. Work with school leadership team to create time during school year for teacher training in teaming skills.				
2. Work with school leadership team to develop collaborative interdisciplinary teams.				
C. Develop professional learning and growth culture in the school.				
1. Coach and mentor teacher leaders.				
2. Train teachers in research-based instructional strategies.				

Table B.3. Sample Professional Learning and Growth Plan for District-Level Leaders

Date: _____
District: _____
School: _____

Name: _____
Position: _____
Evaluator: Superintendent or designee

Performance Rating: _____

Domain 4: Management Competencies
PSEL, 2015, 2, 6, 7, 9, 10
NELP, 2018, 2, 6, 7

Goal: Research, organize, and prepare a bargaining plan for noncertified nonunion staff.

Action Steps	Time	Resources	Person	Evidence
A. Create an organizational plan that will develop a culture that values an ethical and transparent negotiation process. 1. Work with staff leaders to identify terms for the team. 2. Write a plan of action. 3. Identify resources. B. Review the plan with district and school leaders. 1. Discuss strategies. 2. Edit and add changes. 3. Provide professional growth training in research-based negotiation strategies. 4. Present plan to board for approval. 5. Implement plan.	2019–2020 school year	Allocate time for district, school, and staff leaders to work on plan. Share and update as needed.	District leader	1. Staff climate survey. 2. Staff performance goals and evaluations. 3. Staff professional learning and growth plans.

Table B.4. Sample Professional Learning and Growth Plan for School Leaders

Date: _____
District: _____
School: _____

Name: _____
Position: Assistant Principal/Teacher Leader
Evaluator: Principal or designee

Performance Rating:

Domain 1: Leadership Competencies
PSEL, 2015, 2, 4, 6, 7, 10
NELP, 2018, 2, 4, 6, 7
Goal: Increase teacher and student performance.

Action Steps	Time	Resources	Person	Evidence

A. Become a member of the school leadership team.
  1. Accepts invitation to become a member of the school leadership team.
  2. Attends meetings and participates in decision-making.
  3. Conducts action research to improve teacher effectiveness.
B. Supervise classroom teachers.
  1. Coach and mentor classroom teachers.
  2. Conduct formal and informal observations.
  3. Provide professional growth training in research-based instructional strategies.
  4. Provide professional training in the use of assessments and analysis of data for school and district improvement.
	2019–2020 school year	District and school budget allocations to pay school leadership team members for analysis of data and development of the school professional learning and growth plan during the summer.
		
		District funds for release time to attend meetings and coach, mentor, and train teachers.
			Principal
			Teacher
				1. Student performance data from last school year reported at August board meeting.
				
				2. Student performance goals presented at August board meeting.
				
				3. Calendar of training sessions and observation of teachers.
				
				4. School professional learning and growth plans.

Index

About the Authors

Kimberly T. Strike, PhD, is professor of education and coordinator of doctoral programs at Southern Wesleyan University in Central, South Carolina. She has provided services to public, parochial, choice, and charter schools and continues to work with various educational and service programs through local, national, and international channels to advance practice and policy for high-quality programs, development of effective leaders, and effective use of teacher leaders. Among her accomplishments is receipt of the Albert Nelson Marquis Lifetime Achievement Award (2019), PDK's Distinguished Leader in Education Award (2007), and service as an Educational Ambassador to China (2005).

Paul Sims, PhD, is an associate professor and chair of the Department of Leadership at Concordia University-Chicago. Dr. Sims teaches courses on leadership and leadership theories and provides workshops on curriculum, instruction and assessment, and professional learning communities in both the Chicago area and Beijing, China. Prior to university life, he was a teacher, dean of students, and principal in high schools in the Chicagoland area.

Susan L. Mann is currently adjunct professor in the Department of Leadership at Concordia University-Chicago. Susan's expertise in leadership, mentoring, and academic coaching was honed during her lengthy professional career in school leadership as a principal in the northwest suburbs of Chicago.

Robert Wilhite, EdD, is currently the dean of the College of Graduate Studies at Concordia University-Chicago. He teaches classes focusing on the areas of instructional leadership, supervision, school improvement, school change processes, ethics, and legal issues for school districts. Among his research interests are school improvement processes, leadership models and styles, literacy and reading, curriculum, and instruction. He has served as an elementary, middle school, and high school principal; assistant superintendent of instruction; and superintendent of schools.